THE FIRST CHRISTIANS

THE FIRST CHRISTIANS

Their Beginnings, Writings, and Beliefs

EDUARD LOHSE

Translated by
M. EUGENE BORING

FORTRESS PRESS   PHILADELPHIA

This book is a translation of *Die Urkunde der Christen: Was steht im Neuen Testament?* by Eduard Lohse copyright © 1979 by Kreuz Verlag, Stuttgart, Germany.

Biblical quotations, unless otherwise noted, are from the Revised Standard Version of the Bible, copyrighted 1946, 1952, © 1971, 1973 by the Division of Christian Education of the National Council of the Churches of Christ in the U.S.A., and are used by permission. (An asterisked biblical reference indicates that the translator has preserved the nuances of the German rendering of biblical texts.)

Library of Congress Cataloging in Publication Data

Lohse, Eduard, 1924–
   The first Christians.

   Translation of: Die Urkunde der Christen.
   1. Bible, N.T.—Criticism, interpretation, etc.
2. Christianity—Origin. I. Title.
BS2364.2.L6313   225.6   82–7454
ISBN 0–8006–1646–4   AACR2

9595F82   Printed in the United States of America   1–1646

CONTENTS

The New Testament is a collection of writings that show what the first Christians believed and preached—a faith and message by which the church was established and sustained. These writings unanimously testify to the gospel of God's grace, which in Christ is extended to all people of the world. In Christ the Word of God was revealed, a Word that is always conveyed through words spoken by human beings. That Word, preached in a variety of ways, is to be heard wherever the good news of God's grace is proclaimed. It is this news, this gospel, that is the heart and center of Scripture, giving unity to all its parts.

Eduard Lohse

1

GOD'S AGENT

The Center of the New Testament

JESUS OF NAZARETH

All the writings of the New Testament speak of Jesus of Nazareth. Without him, none of the Gospels or early Christian letters would have been written. But not a line has been preserved which he himself wrote. Everything that we know about him was written by other people, the ones on whom he had made such a strong impression that they became his followers. Who is this man? What is reported about him? What do we know of the world in which he lived?

He bore a biblical name, the Hebrew name "Joshua" ("the Lord saves"), which was rendered as "Jesus" in Greek. He came from Nazareth, a small, out-of-the-way village in Galilee. Although northern Palestine had been part of the ancient territory of Israel, for centuries many Greek merchants and business people had also lived in this land. Thus there existed in Galilee settlements of people who spoke the Greek language alongside those of the Jews, who spoke Aramaic. Hebrew, the language of the Bible, was hardly used in daily conversation. Only the scribes spoke Hebrew, which they often used in their long discussions concerning the meaning of particular biblical words. Jesus spoke Aramaic as his mother tongue, but from his early years he would have heard Hebrew read in the synagogue. Thus he would also have been acquainted with the language of the Hebrew Bible. Presumably he also could have understood enough Greek to enable him to converse with Greek-speaking people, but, in fact, he came from a purely Jewish family. The Greek immigrants had never settled in the barren highlands of Galilee. They preferred the fertile plains and seacoast. Thus a purely Jewish population had been preserved in

9

the pathless hill country. From his childhood on, then, Jesus grew up as a Jew in a Jewish environment, learning to read and interpret the ancient Scriptures.

Nazareth was a small, almost unknown village. The place was not significant enough to be mentioned in any contemporary literature. "Can anything good come out of Nazareth?" (John 1:46). This question is not surprising, for how could a man who was expected to be respected and obeyed suddenly appear from a village which no one had ever heard of? Moreover, Jesus' parents were plain, unassuming people. In Nazareth people were acquainted with his family, which was supported by the father's work as a carpenter. Jesus' brothers and sisters were also known (Mark 6:3). More precise information concerning his family and home town has simply not been preserved.

Only in the Gospel of Luke is the story told of Jesus' parents making a trip to Bethlehem just before the child's birth, in order to be registered in the tax rolls. The emperor Augustus had decreed that all residents must register ("be enrolled") in their home towns (Luke 2:1–20). That such procedures were imposed on the whole Roman empire is not mentioned elsewhere in other ancient documents of the times. We do have information concerning individual provinces, however, indicating that everyone in the province of Judea was required to be registered for tax purposes. We know that in the year A.D. 6 the Jewish ruler Archelaus, a son of Herod, had mismanaged things so badly that he was removed from office by the emperor. Judea and Samaria were placed under the direct command of the Roman governor of Syria. This resulted in the new governor's ordering a registration of the whole population for tax purposes, with each person required to declare his or her home town and financial circumstances. But Galilee, the northern section of the country, continued to be subject to the government of Herod Antipas, another son of King Herod. Thus Jesus' home town was not affected by this decree. Luke's portrayal is therefore to be explained as follows: Luke has extended the report of a tax registration in one country to the whole Roman Empire, and has thereby provided a framework which is intended to emphasize the setting of the birth of Jesus in world history. The emperor Augustus set the whole known world in motion, so that Jesus' parents would travel from Nazareth to Bethlehem, and Jesus would be born in the same city from which David came. According to the prophetic promise, the king who would appear at the end of time would also come from Bethlehem (Mic. 5:2–6). Thus the Christmas story does not represent a biographical account, but is a story, a narrative determined by theological motives. It intends to show that Jesus is "the anointed one" of God in whom the prophetic promises find fulfillment.

Palestine at this time was subject to the supremacy of the Romans, who in the middle of the first century B.C. had brought the whole of the Near East under their control. In a few countries such as Syria and Judea, Roman governors ruled directly. Elsewhere, there were indigenous rulers who exercised a limited authority in their own region, subject to the approval of the Roman emperor. This explains why there were different political arrangements in the northern and southern sections of the country in the time of Jesus: Galilee was ruled by the Jewish prince Herod Antipas, while Samaria and Judea were subject to the Roman governor. And the governor administered the country for most of the year from Caesarea on the coast, only making an appearance now and then in the ancient capital, Jerusalem. The Romans, in fact, did not wish to provoke the Jews unnecessarily by reminding them of who actually ruled the land. Furthermore, all Jews knew themselves to be bound to the Temple, the holy place in Jerusalem. Many of them made pilgrimages to the Holy City at the time of the great festivals in the spring and fall of the year. On such occasions the governor also moved to Jerusalem with a detachment of combat-ready troops and took up residence in the former palace of the king, so as to be able to respond to any unrest or riot.

When Jesus was about thirty years old, he began his public ministry. It is only from this brief period of his work in Galilee and Jerusalem that reports have been preserved. His ministry began in an encounter with John the Baptist. John preached on the edge of the wilderness near the Jordan river, and baptized all who responded to his call. According to the Gospel of Luke (3:1–2), John appeared in the fifteenth year of the reign of the emperor Tiberius, that is, in the year A.D. 28/29. But John's ministry came to an early end. Herod Antipas, ruler of Galilee and part of the territory east of the Jordan, had him arrested and executed, for he had been angered by John's preaching of repentance. Herod Antipas had first married a daughter of the king of the Nabateans, but later took as his wife Herodias. She had been married to his half brother, a member of the Herodian family of whom nothing further is known. This was a transgression of the divine command which prohibited a man from taking his brother's wife (Lev. 18:16; 20:21). He had simply sent his first wife back to her father in the Nabatean kingdom. John had held up this wrong plainly before the eyes of the king. For this reason John was thrown into prison and hounded by the fiercely hostile Herodias. She did not rest until John had been killed. The Gospels refer to these events, though the first husband of Herodias is erroneously named Philip (Mark 6:17–29).

Jesus took up the call of John the Baptist, "The kingdom of God is at hand; repent . . ." (Mark 1:15). He did not remain in the wilderness, however, but traveled through the villages and towns, preaching in the synagogues, and restricted his ministry to the area of Palestine populated by Jews. Of course he incidentally came into contact with individual Gentiles who lived in Galilee. But he did not enter those localities populated only by Gentiles, for he knew himself to be sent to Israel. By no means did he associate only with the religious people, rather he also went to those people with whom no pious person was willing to associate: to sinners who had openly transgressed God's law. Indeed, he did not even turn away from prostitutes, but to them as well as to all other people, Jesus declared that God is near, that he wants to show mercy to them and rebuild their lives from the ground up. God's love is there for everyone, but especially for those who need it most.

Jesus' life style created quite a stir. Many people raised objections, but others left everything behind and followed him. Of course, it was not at all unusual in Palestine for a teacher to gather a circle of students around him. But the students were expected to apply for acceptance by the teacher. The teacher examined the applicants to determine whether they were capable of mastering the course of study. The student received instruction for several years, while living in close association with the master. When the teacher finally decided that his student had successfully completed the course of study and was now capable of making independent decisions, he declared him to be a rabbi—"a teacher"—and released him from his school. The relation between Jesus and those who followed him as students or disciples was completely different. It was not they who had sought out Jesus and applied for admission into his school. Rather, Jesus took the initiative, approaching this or that person with the challenge: "Follow me" (Mark 1:17; 2:14). This call alone was the basis of the relationship between Jesus and his followers. Those who were affected by this call left behind everything they possessed and followed Jesus. Even family ties did not hold them back (Matt. 10:37//Luke 14:26). But others did not follow Jesus, because his call seemed to them to be an unreasonable demand (Mark 10:17–22//Matt. 8:19–22//Luke 9:57–62). Nor did Jesus call disciples in order to establish a school. He did not teach them with the goal of making them into teachers who could one day take over the place of the master. Rather he invited people into his community of followers in order that they might share everything with him, including his cross. Thus his disciples were to be like "brothers" to each other, and were never to let themselves be called "rabbi," like the Jewish teachers (Matt. 23:8). Whoever follows Jesus must be ready to accept suffering and death (Mark 8:34–35). The disciples' commission reads: "But as for you, go and proclaim the kingdom of God" (Luke 9:60).

If Jesus' public behavior seemed to be very much like that of a respected Scripture scholar (scribe), it was nonetheless immediately apparent that he was fundamentally different: Jesus did not teach as if he were a scribe. Scribes weighed arguments and counterarguments against each other. Jesus taught with authority (Mark 1:27//Matt. 7:29) and provoked questions: What kind of authority is this? Where did he get it? (Mark 11:28). Who is Jesus of Nazareth? People sought to compare him with different models. Some thought that in him John the Baptist had reappeared (Mark 8:28), that is, that the man whom Herod Antipas once executed had risen from the dead (Mark 6:14). Others remembered the ancient expectation that at the end of time the prophet Elijah would reappear and gather together the scattered tribes of Israel (Mark 8:28). Some saw Jesus as one of the prophets (Mark 8:28). But those who found themselves called together as his people—the first Christian communities—said, "He is the Messiah."

CHRIST

"You are the Christ"—thus Peter responded to the question directed to the circle of Jesus' disciples: "But who do you say that I am?" (Mark 8:29). The Greek word "Christ" means "the anointed one," as does "Messiah" in Aramaic. In ancient Israel the king was inducted into his office by an anointing ceremony (1 Sam. 10:1). Thereby the king was solemnly invested with sovereign power. In the past, for example, under King David, Israel had experienced an age of splendor. That age was remembered and adopted by the pious Jews as a model for their hope of future redemption. Thus the promised ruler, whose advent was awaited by the Jews, was called the Son of David. The more bitter the Roman domination was perceived to be, all the more did the pious turn their thoughts to the future, to the longed-for reversal of things: God would raise up his anointed ruler through whom he would liberate Israel and lead her to glorious splendor. He would give stability to the ruler's house and kingdom, and establish his throne forever. As God had once equipped and strengthened David (2 Sam. 7:11–16), so he also would fill the messianic king—"the anointed one"—with power and enable him to purify Jerusalem and smash the enemy with his rod of iron. Then this messiah would reign as a righteous king. God himself would instruct him as to how Israel should live according to his command. Thus every Jew daily included a petition in his prayer to God: "Lord, our God, in your great compassion have mercy on Israel, your people, and on Jerusalem, your city, and on Zion, the dwelling place of your glory, and on your Temple, and on your dwelling place, and on the kingship of the house of David, your righteous Messiah. Praise be to you, Lord, God of David, who builds Jerusalem."

Jesus of Nazareth is the Christ, the Messiah—this was the confession of the first Christians. What does that mean? Jesus himself resolutely rejected any illusory expectation that he would attempt to change the political conditions with violence. He did not want to be a king, not a ruler like David. So what then is meant, when he is nevertheless called the Messiah? He is not called the Messiah in the sense of the Jewish expectations directed toward the coming messianic king. Yet on his cross an inscription was placed: "The King of the Jews" (Mark 15:26). Thereby the old title, which referred to God's anointed one, received a completely new meaning. The evangelist Mark emphasizes this sense of the title Messiah when, immediately after Peter's confession that Jesus is the Messiah, he quotes Jesus' instruction: "The Son of man must suffer many things, and be rejected by the elders and the chief priests and the scribes, and be killed, and after three days rise again" (Mark 8:31).

The *Son of man* was another title for the one sent by God: the one who is to appear at the end of time as the one commissioned by God to pass judgment over all people (Dan. 7:13; Mark 13:26). This title is also applied to Jesus of Nazareth and thereby receives an entirely new meaning, just as in the case of the title messianic king. No longer does the title allude to an appearance in power and glory, but of lowliness and misery, of suffering, death, and resurrection. In this event—so the Christian message affirms—the great reversal has happened, through which the course of history is fundamentally transformed. That is why Jesus is named the Christ, the Messiah, in whom the fulfillment of what the prophets have promised takes place. In the Greek-speaking world, however, the meaning of the title "Christ" was misunderstood. People assumed that it was a proper name, and thus spoke of "Jesus Christ." In order to explain the meaning of the title, that he is the one sent and authorized by God, other expressions such as "Lord" or "Son of God" were used to point out the sovereign authority of the crucified and risen Christ.

The messianic confession of the Christian community took up prophetic affirmations which had played no role in the dominant messianic expectation of that time. The Psalms repeatedly speak of a pious supplicant who cries out to his God in his extreme distress and affliction. Struck by bitter suffering, he says: "My God, my

God, why hast thou forsaken me?" (Ps. 22:1). "All who see me mock at me, they make mouths at me, they wag their heads; 'He committed his cause to the Lord; let him deliver him' " (Ps. 22: 7–8). "They divide my garments among them, and for my raiment they cast lots" (Ps. 22:18). But the afflicted one knows how to place his confidence in God alone: "But thou, O Lord, be not far off! O thou my help, hasten to my aid!" (Ps. 22:19). His enemies have directed gross insults at him: "They gave me poison for food, and for my thirst they gave me vinegar to drink" (Ps. 69:21). Still, even in his ultimate distress he remains certain that God stands by his side: "Into thy hand I commit my spirit; thou hast redeemed me, O Lord, faithful God" (Ps. 31:5). What had been said in Isaiah 53 about the suffering and death of the servant of God was now read with a new sensitivity and awareness: "Surely he has borne our griefs and carried our sorrows" (Isa. 53:4). "But he was wounded for our transgressions, he was bruised for our iniquities; upon him was the chastisement that made us whole, and with his stripes we are healed" (v. 5). "The Lord has laid on him the iniquity of us all" (v. 6). "They made his grave with the wicked and with a rich man in his death" (v. 9). "He, my servant, the righteous one, will create righteousness for many; for he bears their sins" (v.11*). "He shall have the strong as his spoil, because he gave up his life to death, and was numbered with the transgressors; yet he bore the sin of many, and made intercession for the transgressors" (v. 12*).

In light of these Old Testament passages, the first Christians were able to comprehend what had happened in the suffering and death of Jesus of Nazareth. Here they found the images which enabled them to describe the meaning of this event. They appropriated the biblical expressions presented to them in the Psalms and prophetic Scriptures and used them in their Christian preaching. They summarized the message of the gospel in concise formulas, which were to be firmly impressed in the mind of each person, in order to preserve the essential points—the core—of the Christian proclamation. The apostle Paul refers to one of these formulas in his first letter to the church in Corinth. In quoting it, he specifically points out that he himself had received it as an item of tradition at the time when he became a Christian—only a few years after Jesus' crucifixion. It reads:

For I delivered to you as of first importance what I also received, that Christ died for our sins in accordance with the scriptures, that he was buried, that he was raised on the third day in accordance with the scriptures, and that he appeared to Cephas, then to the twelve (1 Cor. 15:3–5).

This statement declares who the Christ is: not a glorious, conquering king, but the suffering and dying servant of God, despised and defeated. As though he were some criminal, he had been put to death and thrown into a grave. But this event breaks into the present and directly addresses the hearer of the message. Christian preaching therefore constantly takes the form of a direct address which does not allow one to remain a spectator, but demands a decision. The recipients of this message thus find themselves addressed in an extraordinary way, which not only today, but already in earliest times must have had surprising effects. Namely, the recipients are addressed as "sinners," for that is what Paul declares: Christ died for our sins.

Alienation from God, the result of human guilt, is the reason why God's anointed one had to suffer and die. But at the same time, the goal to which his path of suffering was intended to lead is identified. He did for us what we could not do for ourselves. He bore on his own shoulders the guilt heaped up by humanity, so that he was completely covered by this heavy burden. For, as Paul says, God "made him to be sin who knew no sin, so that in him we might become the righteousness of God" (2 Cor. 5:21). He drank the cup of suffering to the dregs, so that we no longer have to drink it. That he traveled this bitter road to the very end is emphasized by the reference to his grave, "that he was buried." He died and was placed in a grave, just as we all must die and be buried.

But how could it happen that the Messiah did not appear in glory and power, but that he had to die the death of a criminal? The Christian proclamation answered that it happened according to the will of God. That is, the Scriptures were turned to for support, with the result that the whole Old Testament was appropriated as a witness for the truth of the message about Christ. When "the

Scriptures'' are mentioned in the New Testament, reference is not made to particular passages; rather the Scripture as a whole is understood as testimony about Christ and on his behalf. The message about Christ is therefore the key which opens the door to the right understanding of the Old Testament as a whole. By the same token, the meaning of Jesus' passion can only be understood with the help of Scripture. Thus because Christians perceived in Jesus' death and resurrection the proof of the infinite love of God by which their lives were transformed and renewed, they constantly were compelled to tell the story of how Christ had suffered, died, and been raised from the dead.

THE CROSS

Along with many other pilgrims, Jesus and his disciples journeyed to Jerusalem in order to celebrate Passover in the Holy City. In the spring of each year the Jewish community remembered Israel's exodus from Egypt, God's marvelous liberation of his people. Jesus' ministry in Galilee had met much opposition among the scribes and scrupulous religious people. Now he was faced with a decision that had to be made in Jerusalem. That Jesus clearly understood the seriousness of an imminent confrontation is indicated by his words, "It cannot be that a prophet should perish away from Jerusalem" (Luke 13:33), for Jerusalem had always killed the prophets, and stoned those sent to her (Matt. 23:37). The gospels themselves report that Jesus had solemnly announced to his disciples what awaited him in Jerusalem:

> Behold, we are going up to Jerusalem; and the Son of man will be delivered to the chief priests and the scribes, and they will condemn him to death, and deliver him to the Gentiles; and they will mock him, and spit on him, and scourge him, and kill him; and after three days he will arise (Mark 10:33–34).

In these words the evangelists combine Jesus' own announcement with a concise report of the events which took place in Jerusalem. They thereby intended to show that God's will was fulfilled in Jesus' way of suffering. It must happen in the way announced beforehand, and not otherwise. The individual way stations of the passion are summarized tersely: Jesus and his disciples traveled to Jerusalem. There he was delivered into the hands of the high priests and scribes. He was condemned to death and handed over to the Gentiles, that is, the Romans. They mocked him, spat on him, scourged him, and killed him. But after three days he was raised from the dead.

Jesus was arrested at night. A disturbance among the people was to be avoided if at all possible. He was taken immediately to a hearing before the high priest, scribes, and elders of the city. The report which the evangelists give of these proceedings makes it clear that the decision to get rid of the troublesome man from Nazareth had been made beforehand. But there was some embarrassment in trying to find legitimate grounds on which he could be pronounced guilty (Mark 14:53–65). Nothing was accomplished by bringing in eyewitnesses who did not agree. Obviously, a key role was played by the allegation that Jesus had said, "I will destroy this temple that is made with hands, and in three days I will build another, not made with hands" (Mark 14:58). From this charge we may infer that the debate between Jesus and his opponents had come to a head during a conflict in the Temple. Jesus had driven out the money-changers and merchants who conducted their business with pilgrims and visitors within its sacred precincts. He wanted to restore the Temple as a place for prayer and worship. The harshness with which Jesus acted was reminiscent of the sharp criticism directed by the Old Testament prophets against the temple cult. Thus Jeremiah had addressed his contemporaries with the word of God: "Has this house, which is called by my name, become a den of robbers in your eyes?" (Jer. 7:11). Like the prophet, Jesus objected to people's tendency to use the worship of God for their own selfish goals. The words and actions of Jesus were directed not against the money-changers and merchants alone, but especially against those who bore the responsibility for the misuse of God's house. The high priests obviously perceived that Jesus' attack was directed against them. Thus they decided to get rid of him. Only their fear of the crowds who followed Jesus kept them, at first, from carrying out their decision (Mark 11:18–19).

The evangelists report that the high priest discontinued the interrogation of the witnesses and directed the crucial question to Jesus himself: "Are you the Christ, the Son of the Blessed?" (Mark 14:61). Jesus answered in the affirmative, which resulted in his being pronounced guilty. By the way they tell the story, the evangelists intend to make clear what are the issues that separate followers of Jesus from his opponents. Who is this Jesus who goes the way to the cross? Does he speak in the name of God? Or does he violate the honor of the Most High? Obviously, the members of the highest Jewish court came to a speedy and unanimous decision to put Jesus to death. But under the prevailing political conditions it was not possible for them to carry out this decision themselves. Since Judea and Jerusalem were subject to the oversight of the Roman governor, the final authority lay in his hand. Therefore Jesus must be brought before the governor with a charge which would convince the Romans, since only the governor could pronounce and execute the death sentence.

The Roman governor gave Jesus only a brief trial. The unanimous testimony of the evangelists is that Pilate asked Jesus, "Are you the King of the Jews?" (Matt. 27:11//Mark 15:2//Luke 23:3). This question reflects the accusation made by the Jewish authorities when they had delivered Jesus to the Romans. Obviously Jesus was delivered to the Romans as a politically suspicious person whose preaching had evoked a dangerous unrest among the population. Thus the charge that he had claimed to be King of the Jews could be based on an intentional perversion of his message concerning the kingdom of God. By interpreting Jesus' message in a political sense, they sought to categorize Jesus among the revolutionaries who repeatedly rose up against the Roman occupation and appealed for violent resistance. The governor had to condemn and execute such people. So Pilate would not have hesitated long to strike down a politically suspicious man by having him crucified. He had assumed his office as governor in A.D. 26. Contemporary reports portray him as a hard man, who exercised his office with greed and cruelty. After ten years in office he lost his position when his oppressed subjects effectively lodged complaints against him with his superior officer in Syria. A ruthless person such as Pilate would not have given a second thought to granting the request of the Jewish authorities and having Jesus executed. And so Jesus was found guilty of claiming to be the King of the Jews (Mark 15:2–10).

After the sentence had been pronounced, Jesus was led away, flogged, and ridiculed. The Roman soldiers often made cruel sport of those who had been condemned to death. They ridiculed Jesus as though he were a king. They dressed him in royal garments, so that they could mockingly honor him and then make their abuse of him all the more cruel. Then he was led away and brought to the place of execution. From the former royal palace, in which the governor was temporarily residing, it was only a short distance to the site for the crucifixion—outside the city walls. The crucifixion took place in full view of the city. The curious, who always turn up on such occasions, could observe the event from the city wall and hurl their sarcastic insults at the condemned. A stake had previously been set in the ground. A crossbeam was then attached to it, which the condemned man himself had had to carry. The Romans had become acquainted with this gruesome manner of execution in the Orient. Crucifixion served to inflict a horrifying death on those who had been condemned from among the subject populations and slaves. Roman citizens could not be executed in this shameful manner. The condemned would often hang on the cross for several days, dying slowly and in agony. Jesus himself had been so weakened by the scourging that he did not have to suffer so long. After a few hours, he uttered a loud cry and died (Mark 15:37). The evangelists report that his last words were a sentence from Psalm 22: "My God, my God, why hast thou forsaken me?" (Mark 15:34). These words express the terrible bitterness of suffering which Jesus had to endure. Nevertheless, just as the suffering righteous man in the depths of distress lifts up a prayer to God (in Psalm 22), so Jesus submits to the will of his God.

A few friends and followers managed to have the body released to them for burial. They placed the body in a burial chamber and rolled a stone in front of the entrance in order to barricade it against intruders and wild animals. No further details are given about the location of the grave. It is simply reported that Jesus was taken down from the cross and placed in a tomb. In sum, he endured his lot as the Suffering Servant of God—to the very end—and in the end was buried among the wicked (Isa. 53:9).

Jesus died the death which was reserved for criminals and outcasts. In the Roman Empire the cross was a mark of disgrace. People were ashamed to speak of human life coming to such an end. Was not death on the cross a clear indication that the way of life which led to it was utterly discredited? Thus Christians often had to endure insult when they spoke of Jesus' cross. Not only to Greeks and Romans, who placed value on persuasive philosophical arguments, but also to Jews, who were interested in God's law and commandment, it seemed inconceivable that God's anointed one should turn out to be the crucified one. Many Christians were hesitant to tell the story of Jesus' cross to other people. So in the early days of the church the cross was not used as a Christian symbol because it evoked too much misunderstanding among outsiders. Only after the emperor Constantine put an end to the persecution of Christians at the beginning of the fourth century A.D. did the sign of the cross, now understood as a symbol of victory, find widespread use in the Roman Empire.

"We preach the Crucified One as the Christ"—thus says the Apostle Paul, and continues: "a stumbling block to Jews and folly to Gentiles, but to those who are called, both Jews and Greeks, Christ the power of God and the wisdom of God" (1 Cor. 1:23–24*). It was precisely the crucified one who was proclaimed as the resurrected one. Because he had been raised from the dead, therefore his death did not signify the tragic end of a noble life; rather his cross creates life and salvation (1 Cor. 15:17). Christ died once, and therefore once and for all, in order to gain victory over death. Therefore, Christians cannot speak only of Jesus' cross but must at the same time also speak of his resurrection.

RESURRECTION

"Christ . . . was raised on the third day in accordance with the scriptures . . . he appeared to Cephas, then to the twelve" (1 Cor. 15:4–5)—according to the earliest Christian proclamation. The Scripture is again called upon to support this message. No particular text is named, but the Old Testament as a whole is claimed as evidence for the truth of the Christian proclamation. This message is derived from witnesses to whom the risen Lord appeared—from Cephas and the Twelve, who saw the Lord. What do they say concerning the resurrection of Jesus Christ?

The names of those who witnessed the resurrected Lord are offered as a guarantee of the truth of their message. They vouch for the message which they personally hand on. Only the event itself is named: the resurrected one appeared to them. Beyond that, no details are given. Where the appearance to Cephas occurred, whether in Jerusalem or Galilee, is not mentioned. Nor is there any hint expressed as to where the risen Lord encountered the Twelve. It is important to note, however, that there is no reference to visions; rather testimony is given to an event which is understood as an act of God. The disciples had of course fled from the crucifixion, disappointed and despairing. Despite their feelings, God acted to change their situation in a fundamental way. He raised up Christ. But the resurrected Lord was certified as the living one to the disciples. By contrast, in the ancient world there are several stories reporting that a dead person was restored to life in a marvelous way. But the content of the Easter story represents a very different message from such stories, for Christ was not simply restored to the life which he had previously lived. If the resurrection of Jesus were merely the return of a dead person to life, then it would fall in that category of events which one can investigate and prove or disprove. Moreover, if someone returns from death into our world of living, then death itself would not really be overcome. For such a "resurrection" one would remain subject to the terms and conditions of our own existence and would ultimately have to die again. But the resurrection of Jesus Christ is proclaimed as the victory over death itself. That God raised him from the dead means one thing: death is deprived of its power and life triumphs.

This message is not rightly understood if one attempts either to prove or to disprove it. One can, however, subject the events which happened immediately before and after it to examination and show that they really happened: Jesus' way to the cross—and the flight of the disciples, who were so terrified that they went to pieces, but then suddenly reappeared full of confidence and joy. How did this fundamental transformation take place? The Christian proclamation answers the question clearly: God raised Christ from the dead. The risen Lord appeared to his disciples and thereby made them his messengers. They had been full of doubt and hesitation. But when the resurrected one presented himself to be recognized as the living Lord, no longer could they ponder about the possible truth of the resurrection. Those to whom the resurrected one appeared were themselves caught up in the resurrection event and were called into service as his witnesses. From then on they could be nothing other than messengers of the resurrected Lord. Using words from early Christian preaching, Paul says, "If you confess with your lips that Jesus is Lord and believe in your heart that God raised him from the dead, you will be saved" (Rom. 10:9). Believing that God raised Jesus from the dead is identified with the confession that he is the Lord. Whoever can say that is a Christian. The Easter message authenticates itself as true, in that the testimony delivered by the witnesses grips the hearers and creates the response of faith to which it is directed. For in the preaching of his messengers the risen one speaks his own word.

The Easter message is illustrated in the gospels in a series of stories which portray the encounters between the risen Lord and his disciples. Whether the stories are about the narrow circle of disciples, or two travelers, a single individual, or a group of women, the constant factor which they represent is the compelling power with which the Easter message grips the lives of people, filling them with the assurance that Jesus is Lord. Thus the evangelist Luke tells how two disciples were walking from Jerusalem to Emmaus on the first Easter Sunday morning (Luke 24:13–35). Filled with despair, they are discussing the events of recent days. Jesus' life had come to a terrible end on the cross. Then they were joined by a third person, who being surprised at their dejection asked why. He (Jesus) told them they were foolish, uncomprehending, and too dull to believe the words of the prophets. For if they had only opened the Scriptures, they would certainly understand that the story of Jesus could not have turned out any other way. It must happen according to God's will, that the Christ should suffer in order to enter into his glory. This the prophets had already known.

During this conversation—so the story continues—they reach their destination. The two travelers invite the stranger to come in and stay with them. They sit together at the table for the common meal. The guest takes the bread, blesses it, breaks it, and gives it to them. Then the eyes of both men are opened, and they recognize the stranger, and he vanishes out of their sight. Astonished, they ask each other, "Did not our hearts burn within us while he talked to us on the road, while he opened to us the Scriptures?" They arise at once and return to Jerusalem, where they find the disciples gathered together, and hear the news from them: "The Lord has risen indeed, and has appeared to Simon [Peter]." Then they tell what they had experienced "on the road," how they had recognized the risen Lord as he broke the bread for the common meal.

This story represents a vivid portrayal of the earliest preaching on the meaning of the Easter event. It incorporates a motif familiar to many peoples of the ancient world: the deity himself comes in human form, unrecognized, and encounters believers and unbelievers alike. For example, according to Genesis 18, three men once visited Abraham in Mamre, were hospitably received by him, and promised him that despite his old age he would become the father of a son. One of these three men was the Lord himself, who gave his promise to Abraham. Another tale was told among Greeks and Romans of how Jupiter and Minerva had once visited a village, disguised in human form. Everywhere they found closed doors. No one opened a door to them, except an elderly couple, Philemon and Baucis, who received the unrecognized travelers with friendly hospitality and entertained them as well as they could. During the meal, however, the wine was miraculously increased. Thus the gods allowed the old couple to recognize them and commanded them to follow them out to a hillside. There they watched as the village below was destroyed. Only their hut, in which the gods had found lodging, remained standing, and it was transformed into a temple for the gods. The wish of the old couple—to be caretakers of the sacred places for the gods and then to be permitted to die together—was granted them.

The Emmaus story tells how the risen Lord appeared unrecognized at the side of the two travelers. But in the very moment in which he was recognized, he disappeared. The motif of the appearance of the deity, at first not perceived but then made manifest in faith, serves to convey the message vividly. The story shows how faith in the risen one originates. The Lord comes to two men, accompanies them unrecognized on their way, and is testified to as the living Christ by the word of the Scripture.

This means that only in the encounter with the risen Christ is the meaning of Scripture as a whole disclosed. The Bible must therefore be seen from the point of view of its goal. Then from every book will be heard the one word of God concerning Christ. He is the goal and the center, the heart of the entire Scripture. When it is rightly read and interpreted, then the word of the risen one is heard from it, who as the Lord of the church shares himself with his disciples in the celebration of his communal meal. His community then understands that, according to God's gracious will, the Christ had to suffer, and from suffering enter into his glory. Therefore the church confesses with the apostles: The Lord is risen indeed! God has raised him from the dead!

FOR FURTHER READING

Bornkamm, Günther. *Jesus of Nazareth*. New York: Harper & Row, 1975.

Brown, Raymond. *The Virginal Conception and Bodily Resurrection of Jesus*. New York: Paulist Press, 1973.

Conzelmann, Hans. *Jesus*. Philadelphia: Fortress Press, 1973.

Grollenberg, Lucas. *Jesus*. Philadelphia: Westminster Press, 1979.

Perrin, Norman. *The Resurrection According to Matthew, Mark, and Luke*. Philadelphia: Fortress Press, 1977.

Reumann, John. *Jesus in the Church's Gospels*. Philadelphia: Fortress Press, 1974.

Weber, Hans-Ruedi. *The Cross: Tradition and Interpretation of the Crucifixion of Jesus in the World of the New Testament*. Grand Rapids: Wm. B. Eerdmans, 1978.

Wilckens, Ulrich. *Resurrection*. Atlanta: John Knox Press, 1978.

2

JESUS' WORDS AND DEEDS

The Message of Love

GOD

Who is God? The Bible does not respond to this question with theoretical definitions. It speaks rather of how God acts. God shows who he is through his works. Jesus also speaks in this manner of God, and says: God cares for us, God waits on us, and God comes to us.

God cares for us. Whoever opens his or her eyes and ponders how things happen in nature can see God's own handwriting in the natural world, and that he has created and preserved all things. Just look, so says Jesus: There are the birds in the sky. They neither sow, nor harvest, nor gather into barns. But the heavenly father feeds them anyway. And observe how the lilies grow in the fields. They neither work nor spin. But Solomon in all his glory was not clothed like one of them. So if God takes care of the birds in the sky and clothes the flowers in the fields, will he not do even more for human beings? Jesus said, You should not be anxious and say, What will we eat? What will we drink? What will we wear? For the Gentiles (that is, those who are far from God) set their hearts on such things. But your heavenly father knows everything you need (Matt. 6:24–34*).

Do not be anxious! What does that mean? Of course, people in the Orient of 2000 years ago lived a much more modest and less demanding life than we. They managed to get along with a little food and drink, were satisfied with simple clothing, and did not have to make long-range plans. Nevertheless, Jesus' teaching cannot be adequately explained merely by the differences between the living arrangements of that time and those of our own day. It would be a complete misunderstanding to suppose that Jesus taught a frivolous life style or wanted to encourage a thoughtless approach to everyday life. It is rather a matter of the right attitude toward life. As Jesus put it in another way, no one can add one step to life's journey, no matter how much he or she may worry about it. Despite all medical knowledge, death cannot be finally banned. God sets the end and determines the last hour. Thus everything depends on seeing the tasks of daily life in the right perspective, distinguishing important from unimportant, ultimate from penultimate. The one who knows that life rests in God's hands is freed from the anxiety of having to find the goal and meaning of his or her own life independently of God. Such a person can trustingly receive life as a present from God, and rejoice in the gift which God gives. "Do not be anxious" does not mean anything like "Do not work." Rather it means to place one's trust where it belongs. The person who trusts in God is freed from the anxiety that he or she must alone take charge of the uncertain future by industrious striving. Such a person knows that each day has its own troubles, and can devote himself or herself completely to the present, which has sufficient tasks and challenges of its own. If he or she knows how to assign ultimate and penultimate their proper priorities, then he or she will understand what is meant when Jesus says: "But seek first his kingdom and his righteousness, and all these things shall be yours as well" (Matt. 6:33).

God cares for us, *and he waits on us*. Jesus makes this clear in the story of "The Prodigal Son" (Luke 15:11–32). One day the younger of two sons said to his father: "Father, give me the share of property that falls to me." The father responded to the request, and divided his property between the two sons. The younger son then packed up and moved to a distant land. There he spent his money carelessly, so that it was not long until he had squandered it completely. When a severe famine struck the land he found himself in dire need, but he found a citizen who saved him from dying. This citizen sent him into his fields to feed swine, but the hunger of the prodigal was so great that he longed to fill his stomach with the pods which the swine ate. But no one gave him anything. At that point he remembered who he was and thought to himself: my father has many hired workers who have plenty to eat, and here I am, dying of hunger. I will turn and go to my father, and say, "Father, I have sinned against heaven and before you. I am no longer worthy to be called your son; treat me as one of your hired servants." And so he journeyed home, heading to the house of his father. But while he was still at a distance, his father saw him and had compassion on him. He ran to meet him, embraced him, and kissed him. The father commanded his servants, "Bring quickly the best robe, put it on him, put a ring on his finger, and shoes on his feet. Bring the fatted calf and kill it, let us eat and have a good time. For this my son was dead, and is alive again; he was lost, and is found." And so the party began (15:11–24*).

In those days many young men left poverty-stricken Palestine and sought their fortunes in one of the other countries situated around the Mediterranean. Thus also this young man turned his back on his father's house. He wanted to take destiny into his own hands and no longer have to live under the direction of his father. But in the foreign country everything went wrong. The friends who had gathered around him disappeared when the money was gone. He suddenly found himself in distress. Although swine were considered by Jews to be ritually unclean animals, he must have been glad at least to find a job feeding them, since the alternative was death by starvation. But then he thought the matter over after he came to his senses and decided to return to his father. With this decision he changed the direction of his life. He turned around and headed for home. During the whole time of his absence the father had been waiting for him. Day after day he had been on the lookout for him, hoping perhaps that his son might return. One day, he did not look in vain. While the son was still at a distance, the father recognized the hesitant step of his son. He ran to meet him, took him in his arms, and cried out with joy that his son had come back home—just as if he had been brought back from the dead. Through this story Jesus wants to show that just as this father patiently waited for his son and without reflection or hesitation took him back as his son, so God waits on us. Jesus invites us to join with him in the celebration over the return home of a person who has abandoned his or her false way of life and has come back home— to God.

The father of whom Jesus speaks had two sons. The elder of the two had not left home, but had remained with his father. Just after his younger brother had returned home, as he was coming in from the fields, he heard music and dancing, and learned that in fact his brother had come home, and that their father was throwing a welcome-home party for him. At that the elder son became angry, and would not enter the house. So his father went out and asked him to come in. But he answered his father: "I have already served you these many years, and have never disobeyed your command; but you have never given me a party so that I could have a good time with my friends." Then his father answered him: "My Son, you are always with me, and all that is mine is yours. But you should rejoice and be glad, for this your brother was dead and is alive, he was lost, and is found." (15:25–32*).

The elder son insisted on what he supposed were his rights. He no longer acknowledged his returned brother to be a brother. He only referred to him indirectly: "But when this son of yours came, who has devoured your living with harlots, you killed for him the fatted calf." He was not willing to join the party, for he believed that there was no reason for such a celebration. But the father *also* goes out to the elder son and attempts to win him over: "Your brother has returned home, he who was lost is found again. So you should also join in the celebration and have a good time." With these words of the father, the story ends. It says nothing more about the response of the elder son, whether he might have changed his mind after all.

This story leaves open the question which Jesus wanted to pose to the religious folk of his time. These folk held the opinion that they had fulfilled God's will and thought that they therefore had a claim on God—to be acknowledged and praised by him. With disdain they looked down on those who had transgressed God's commands or those who served the foreign occupation forces as tax collectors. How could Jesus sit at the same table with such people? (Luke 15:1–2). To them Jesus says: God waits for people to change the direction of their lives and come back home.

God comes to us. With this announcement Jesus began his public ministry: "Repent, for the kingdom of heaven is at hand"

(Matt. 4:17). "The kingdom of God is at hand; repent!" (Mark 1:15). The two expressions "kingdom of heaven" and "kingdom of God" have the same meaning. In order not to profane the name of God, pious Jews avoided pronouncing the word "God" at all. Instead, when one wanted to speak of God, a series of other terms were used, for example "heaven." Thus "kingdom of heaven" means nothing more or less than "kingdom of God," the establishment of divine sovereignty. Jesus says, God's kingdom has come near, so near that its dawning already directly affects the present. Because God comes and his arrival is already announced through Jesus, this message must be heard and the necessary conclusions must be drawn from it: leave the false way, repent and turn to God, the God who cares for us, waits on us, and comes to us.

RIGHTEOUSNESS

Jesus speaks in parables to express how the kingdom of God may be compared to everyday life in the world. He thus compares the kingdom to things with which everyone is familiar, or makes contact with events happening at the time. These kingdom stories, told in parable form, are not intended to be interpreted point by point in terms of some underlying meaning. Rather each contains a single decisive point of comparison, which is to be grasped and brought into relationship to the message which Jesus proclaimed: *God's kingdom comes.*

How does God's kingdom come? Jesus answers that the kingdom of God is a miracle: it comes about in a way similar to what happens when a farmer sows seed on the land. Afterwards he goes to bed and rises, day after day. Meanwhile the seed sprouts and grows—without any help from the farmer at all. To this process of growth he is able to contribute nothing. The earth brings forth fruit of itself—first the blade, then the ear, then the full grain in the ear. But when the grain is ripe, he at once lays the sickle to it, because the harvest has come (Mark 4:26–29).

What does this parable intend to say? In the language of the Bible the picture of "the harvest" had been used for ages to characterize God's final intervention and the execution of his judgment. The sickle is used to reap the harvest and bring the grain into the barns (Joel 3:13). In those days, however, growth and ripening were not understood as a natural process, but were attributed to God's wonderful activity. A grain of seed is placed in the earth, where it must die. But God wakes it up to new life and causes blade, ear, and the full grain to appear, until it ripens for harvest. Jesus' parable of seedtime and harvest intends to portray how miraculously God works. The harvest comes, without anyone being able either to delay it or hurry it along. So also God lets his kingdom come—apart from all human effort. The pairing of the two activities—sowing and harvesting—portrays the greatness of the divine miracle. God's kingdom comes, and human activity is no more able to make it arrive than it is able to postpone its coming. In contrast, however, to the way many contemporary faithful Jews expressed their hopes, Jesus did not describe the kingdom as the rule of a messianic king who would strike down the enemy and restore the glory of Israel. Rather, he said that God's kingdom will be a rule of grace. His grace, however, is his righteousness. Jesus explains in other parables what that means.

In "The Parable of the Workers in the Vineyard" (Matt. 20: 1–16) Jesus likens the kingdom of God to the time of the grape harvest. The owner of a vineyard sought to obtain as many workers as possible to help him with the harvest. That is why he went out early to the village market. There he found people standing around without work. He quickly struck an agreement with them, that they should go work in his vineyard and receive one denarius for the day's work, which was the usual wage for a day laborer. In that time, a lamb usually cost about four denarii, so a day laborer earned just about the minimum of what a modest standard of living required. The laborers went to work. Three hours later the owner went to the marketplace and found others who had nothing to do, but were just standing around. He hired them too, and said to them: "You go into the vineyard too, and whatever is right I will give you." By this he meant the usual arrangements by which day laborers are hired. So they agreed to his proposal. At noon and again at three in the afternoon the owner returned to the marketplace. And each time he found people whom he hired with the same understanding. Even at five o'clock—one hour before quitting time—once again he went to the market and again found idle people there. "Why have you been standing around here the whole day?" he asked, and then said to them, "You go work in the vineyard too." So they helped with the harvest for one hour.

When evening came, the owner instructed his manager, "Call the workers together and pay them, and begin with those hired last." The manager did just as he was told. First came the people who had not been hired until late afternoon and had worked only one hour. Each of them received a denarius. Thus when the others were called, they supposed that they would receive more. But each of them too received a denarius. They became angry, grumbled at the owner, and said: "These last have worked only one hour. But you have dealt with them just as with us, and we have worked all day." In their resentment they raised bitter complaints against the owner: "He should have given us more! He can't just treat everybody alike!" Thereupon the owner turned and addressed one of them in a friendly tone: "Friend, I am doing you no wrong; you agreed with me to work for one day for a denarius. That was the contract; I have complied with it exactly. Take what belongs to you and leave. I want to give to this last one as to you. May I not do with my own money as I choose? Or are you grudging because I am generous?" (Matt. 20:1–15*).

The resentment of the laborers who had worked all day and had patiently borne the blistering midday heat is completely understandable. They hold to the justifiable perspective of equal pay for equal work. Whoever had worked only a short time should receive less pay than those who had labored the whole day through. The owner, however, does not accept this argument at all. He appeals rather to the agreement which they had made in the early morning. He held to it exactly and paid the agreed amount without any deductions. He reserves the right to do as he wants with his own money. Thus he had decided to pay those who had been hired last a whole day's pay. They too should receive what one needs for a modest living, no more and no less. Was it not simply their grudging envy which had raised the objection against his behavior? Again the parable ends by leaving the question open. It challenges the hearer to make his or her own judgment. How will this turn out? Must not his or her sense of fair play call for a decision that those who raised objections are right? Or will it be recognized that even the last should receive enough to meet their needs? Jesus' parable intends to say, God gives to all what they need. He gives his grace not in various grades or in different degrees; rather he turns to all in the same way.

The thrust of Jesus' parable becomes all the more clear when it is placed beside a parable used by the Jewish scribes. It is preserved in the *Talmud,* and is first documented in its present written form at the beginning of the fourth century A.D. Since it undoubtedly used the same material on which Jesus' parable is based, a comparison is justified. A very talented young scribe, Rabbi Bun by name, had suddenly died at an early age. His former teachers and colleagues gathered for the burial ceremony. One of them delivered the funeral sermon, which included the following parable. There was once a king who had hired many workers. Two hours after the work had begun the king came to observe how the workers were doing. He found one among them who worked both better and more quickly than all the others. He called him over and took him on a walk until evening. Then came the time for the workers to be paid. Each of the workers received the wage which had been agreed upon. The man who had worked only two hours, and then had strolled around with the king the rest of the day, also received a full day's pay. Thereupon the others complained and raised an objection, "He worked only two hours, why does he receive a full day's pay just as we do?" The king—so the story goes—replied as follows: "Nothing unjust is being done to you. This worker did more in two hours than you did all day. He worked so well and so quickly that in this short time he accomplished at least as much as you did. Thus he receives the full payment." In conclusion, then, the deceased young scholar is eulogized: "So Rabbi Bun, whom we bury today, has accomplished more in the twenty-eight years of his short life than many scholars who live to be a hundred. This is why God has called him so early to himself."

According to this parable God's righteousness has to do with the fact that he rewards each according to his accomplishment. By contrast, in Jesus' parable the decisive factor is not the workers' accomplishment but the generosity of the owner of the vineyard. Because of his own grace the owner pays the last just as much as the first. They have no meritorious accomplishments to point to as the basis for claiming a full day's pay, but they receive what they need for their life as a gift. What will the others say? Will they react with jealousy? They are like the self-secure religious folk who observe with suspicion and resentment how Jesus goes to the despised people with whom no one wanted to associate. Or will they be able to celebrate that no payment according to work will be made, but no one goes away empty? Then they will grasp who God is and how Jesus operates. For God's nature is to be generous, and his righteousness is his grace.

GRACE

"How often must I forgive my brother when he has done something against me? Is seven times enough?" The question comes from Peter. He obviously expresses considerable interest in reconciliation, for whoever is willing to forgive and start over seven times certainly deals graciously with others! But Jesus answers: "I do not say to you seven times, but seventy times seven" (Matt. 18:21–22*). This extravagant number indicates that grace without limit should prevail. This grace cannot be understood as a duty which can be accomplished if one works hard enough; rather, grace grows out of the power of the new life which fills Jesus' disciples.

Jesus tells a parable (Matt. 18:23–35). There was once a king who wanted to settle accounts with his servants, that is, with high officials and governors. When he began the auditing process, one who owed him ten thousand talents of silver was brought before him. An enormous sum! The talent represented the highest monetary unit used in the ancient world. Its value varied from country to country, but averaged about two thousand dollars. The debt would thus total about twenty million dollars. Even when one considers that according to ancient law a governor was considered personally responsible to the king for all the receipts in his whole territory, this amount was unimaginably high at that time. For instance, the Jewish prince Archelaus, who governed Judea and Samaria until A.D. 6, obtained a total of six hundred talents per year from his territory; Herod Antipas, who ruled in the time of Jesus, could only extract two hundred talents per year from his territory. Ten thousand talents represented a sum which no one in that day could have raised. How could such a debt ever be paid back? This lord was angry with the servant who owed him so much, and commanded that he, his wife, his children, and all that he possessed be sold and that the proceeds be used to cover the debt. Yet the price of slaves was so low in the ancient world that the money realized through their sale could hardly begin to pay off such a debt. The command of the lord to sell the debtor and his family signifies nothing other than the expression of his wrath directed against this servant. In his despair the servant fell at his master's feet and implored him, "Have patience with me, and I will pay you everything." In his distress he promised the impossible. His supplication, however, was not without effect on his lord. The lord had mercy on his servant, let him go free, and even released him from the debt.

The story portrays the king and his servants, along with the unheard-of size of the debt, in such a way that the reader senses that the parable is not just describing things as they usually happen. Rather it is suggestive of the relation that exists when human beings live their lives before God. Hopelessly in debt, each one is utterly dependent on God's grace. Yet, God is gracious. He forgives the debt and grants freedom as a gift. But as for those who have been forgiven such a great debt and granted their freedom, how then shall they live?

Jesus' parable continues. The servant whose unpayable debt had been removed unexpectedly went out and came upon one of his colleagues, a man who owed him a hundred denarii. A denarius represented one day's pay for a day laborer (Matt. 20:2). A hundred denarii would thus be about forty dollars—a sum which a man could pay off by devoting some work toward it. But it bears no comparison at all to the size of the debt which the lord had forgiven the first servant, six hundred thousand times higher than the second servant's debt. But what did the creditor do? He seized him by the collar, began to choke him, and yelled: "Pay me everything you owe!" Then his fellow servant fell at his feet and begged him, "Have patience with me, and I will pay you everything." He begged with the same words which his creditor had previously directed to the king to whom he had owed ten thousand talents. In contrast to that plea, however, the promise of the second servant to pay everything is entirely possible. He needs only a little time. But the plea is in vain! The creditor refused to deal patiently with him and immediately had his debtor cast into prison until he paid the balance. When fellow servants saw what had taken place, they were very distressed. So they went and reported to their lord all that had taken place. Then the lord had the first servant brought to him and said to him, "You scoundrel! I forgave you all that debt because you begged me; and should not you have had mercy on your fellow servant, as I had mercy on you?" In his wrath he handed him over to the jailers, until he should pay off the whole ten thousand talents—which of course was impossible. The unmerciful servant was delivered into that torment from which there is no release. Thus the parable concludes with a warning: "So also my heavenly father will do to every one of you, if you do not forgive your brother from your heart" (Matt. 18:23–35*).

Merciful dealing toward others, the parable intends to make clear, grows out of receiving that grace of God by which he "forgives us our debts." "Be merciful, even as your Father is merciful" (Luke 6:36). Then God's will is done. But whoever lets his own selfishness make him blind or deaf to the needs of his brother will be called to account.

God demands an accounting. It is like (according to the parable of Matt. 25:14–30) a rich man who was going on a trip to a foreign country. He called his servants together and entrusted his property to them. To one he gave five talents of silver, to another two, and to a third one, to each according to his competence. The one who had received the five talents proceeded at once to trade with them, and made five talents more. Similarly, the one who had received two talents made an additional two talents. But the one who had received one talent went out, dug a hole in the ground, and hid his master's money in it. After a long time the master returned and called in his servants for an accounting. The first stepped forth and said, "Lord, you delivered five talents to me; I have worked with them and made five talents more." The Lord said to him, "Well done, competent and faithful servant; you have been faithful over a little, I will set you over much. Go on in and have a good time at the party of your lord." Next the two-talent man stepped forward. He also had worked effectively and received the corresponding reward. Finally the third servant appeared and said, "Lord, I knew you to be a hard man. You reap where you do not sow, and gather where you have not threshed. So I was afraid, and went and buried your talent in the ground. See, here you have what belongs to you." But his lord answered him, "You evil and lazy servant! Did you really know that I reap where I do not sow? Then you ought to have invested my money at the bank. Then when I returned, I would have received my own money back with interest. So take the talent from him, and give it to the one who has ten talents. And throw this useless servant into the outer darkness, where there is screaming and gnashing of teeth" (Matt. 25:14–30*).

This parable also mentions the talent, the highest monetary unit, to indicate the gift which the rich man entrusted to his servants. On the basis of this story the word "talent" has received a meaning which remains quite common today. We have adopted it in our language to describe the special ability of a person; we speak, for example, of the talent of an artist. The parable wants to make it clear that each of the servants received a gift, this one more, that one less—each according to his ability. But none went away empty-handed. It is necessary, however, to recognize the gift that is received and to work with it. It is not required that everyone produce the same results. But the one who handles his or her gift irresponsibly is the one who does nothing; he or she lets one's talent lie in the ground, or from fear or stubbornness keeps one's hands in the pockets. From each one is taken away what each has. Excuses are of no avail. For if this servant had really believed that his lord would require an accounting, then he would have known all the more that he was obliged to get something done.

The servants are to be ready for the arrival of their lord. Those who have taken their gifts and put them to work in acts of mercy are ready. These people are able to forget about keeping an account of what they have done, and they will be surprised to hear from the mouth of the Judge: "I was hungry, and you gave me something to eat. I was thirsty, and you gave me something to drink. I was a foreigner, and you accepted me. I was naked, and you gave me something to wear. I was sick, and you visited me. I was in prison, and you came to me" (Matt. 25:35–36*). Astonished, they will ask, "Lord, when did we see you hungry and give you something to eat? Or thirsty, and give you something to drink? When did we see you as a foreigner, and receive you? Or naked and clothe you? When did we see you sick or in prison and visit you?" And the king will answer them, "Truly, I say to you, what you have done for these most insignificant brothers of mine, you have done for me" (Matt. 25:37–40*).

LOVE

Which is the greatest commandment of all? This question, according to the evangelists, was once put to Jesus by a scribe (Mark 12:28–34; cf. Matt. 22:35–40 and Luke 10:25–28). People knew that the books of the Old Testament contained a large number of commandments by which they were supposed to live. In addition to the Ten Commandments, there were prescriptions concerning the proper conduct of the temple worship, concerning the offering of sacrifices, concerning the way of life which is pleasing to God, and much else besides. In explanations which the scribes added to these sections of the Bible, these commandments were elaborated and set forth in a more detailed fashion by supplementary provisions. "Keep the Sabbath day holy" meant that one must be careful not to perform any kind of work on the Sabbath; one may only travel a short distance, in order to participate in the synagogue worship; food for the Sabbath must be prepared the day before, in order that the holy day might not be profaned, and so forth. But which commandments are important for answering the question, "What shall I do to inherit eternal life?" (Luke 10:25)? The discussions of the scribes had led to the conclusion that there were 613 commands and prohibitions in the Law with which one should

comply. But how can one find one's way among so many? Which is
the greatest commandment?

Jesus, according to the Gospel of Luke, gives this answer to the
scribe: "What is written in the Law? How do you read?" (Luke
10:26). He thus refers the questioner to the Bible with which he has
been entrusted. The scribe responds that he finds therein, "You
shall love the Lord your God with all your heart, and with all your
soul, and with all your strength, and with all your mind; and your
neighbor as yourself" (Luke 10:27). In this sentence he combines
two different Old Testament passages in one statement. Deut. 6:5
speaks of the love of God and Lev. 19:18 of love for the neighbor.
That these two commandments belong together was already recognized in contemporary Judaism. For example, a text from that
period declares, "Love the Lord in your whole life, and one
another in honest hearts." Another example: "Love the Lord and
your neighbor; have compassion on the weak and the poor." Thus
a Jewish theologian of that time could certainly have given such an
answer as is formulated in the double commandment of love. It was
known that love for God is not possible without love for the
neighbor, and that love for the neighbor cannot be exercised apart
from true faith in God. They sought, however, one general basic
law which summarized God's demand as simply and clearly as
possible, so that everyone could know what was most important.
And it was found here: "You shall love God, and your neighbor as
yourself." Jesus said, "You have answered right; do this, and you
will live" (Luke 10:28).

How should this commandment to love the neighbor be understood? "Neighbor" is generally understood to refer to those who
belong to one's own people. Members of other nations and cultures
are thus not included in the command to love. One has no relationship with them anyway; one may hate them or fight against them.
In some Jewish religious groups, the boundary was drawn much
more narrowly. The Pharisees accepted into their associations
only those who were willing to adhere strictly to God's commands.
For such pious folk, only those who had accepted this obligation
were considered to be the neighbors to whom one should relate in
love. All others were excluded from the realm in which the com-

mand to love one's neighbor was applicable. The line was drawn even more sharply in the community which had chosen to live at Qumran on the shore of the Dead Sea, so that they could devote themselves wholly to God's commands and live according to his Law, undisturbed by the concerns of city and nation. Their members called themselves "sons of light," because they had resolved, as God's holy combat squad, to lead the fight against darkness. In this spiritual battle, which must be fought to the finish, one must live by the rule "to love all the sons of light, but to hate all the sons of darkness." The statement in Matt. 5:43 refers to this instruction, "You have heard that it was said, 'You shall love your neighbor and hate your enemy.' " Such a statement cannot be found in the Old Testament, but it is found in the teaching of such strict Jews. They defined the love commandment so narrowly that they understood it to include only people with the same religious convictions. All other people were considered enemies, because in their view they did not live according to God's Law with the same zeal. Love was not appropriate to them, but hate was.

"Who is my neighbor?" (Luke 10:29). In the Judaism of Jesus' day that was a question about which there was a variety of opinions which differed strongly with each other: those of the same religious convictions as ours, the members of our religious group, the members of our nation. Where is the boundary to be drawn? How far does God's command apply?

Jesus responded to this question with a story (Luke 10:30–37). A man was traveling down the road from Jerusalem to Jericho. Then as now, this road passes through desert country. It passes through no villages; not even individual houses are located along it. Jerusalem is located in the mountains, about eight hundred meters above sea level. Jericho, however, is located in the depths of the Jordan valley, situated several hundred meters below sea level, which means that the road drops more than twelve hundred meters in its twenty-seven kilometers. On this deserted road travelers who journeyed alone were often attacked and robbed by thieves. This is what happened to a Jew who made his way along this road. Robbers fell on him, stripped him, beat him, and left him lying half dead. Some time later, a priest came along. Obviously he was on his way home, after his time of duty in the Temple in Jerusalem was over. The priesthood was divided into twenty-four sections, each of which was on duty for a week. When the replacements arrived, the priests could return home and live there until they were recalled to service in about six months. Many priests lived with their families in Jericho. When their duty in Jerusalem was over, they looked forward to going back home again. One had no time to be bothered with some man who lay helpless alongside the road. A Levite, who had similarly finished his Temple service, felt the same way about the situation. He too passed on by without attending to the wounded man.

Finally, a Samaritan came along. Jews and Samaritans were bitter enemies. Although the Samaritans also acknowledged the five books of Moses as Holy Scripture, the Jews wanted nothing to do with their northern neighbors and did not recognize them as legitimate worshipers of the God of Israel. Jewish people despised them, did not want to associate with them, and treated them with contempt and hatred. Nevertheless, the Samaritan traveler, when he saw the wounded Jew lying half-dead alongside the road, did not remember all the hateful words which had been shouted at him and the people of his country. He attended to the injured man, cleaned up his wounds with oil and wine, and bound them up. Then he lifted him up onto his own animal, brought him to an inn, and took care of him. The priest and Levite had passed on by, although it was their responsibility to take care of one of their own countrymen. It was a foreigner, who otherwise hardly came in contact with Jews, that came to him, bound up his wounds, and brought him to safety. Which of these three—thus Jesus asks in conclusion—became a neighbor to the man who fell victim to the robbers? The answer can only be: the one who showed mercy. And Jesus said, "Go and do likewise" (Luke 10:37).

The question, "Then, who is my neighbor?" has thus found a new, compelling answer. The question is no longer, "Who is my neighbor?" but "Who became neighbor to the man who fell victim to the robbers?" The thing to consider must therefore be expressed, "To whom do I become neighbor?" Jesus says: All the restrictions which limit the concept of neighbor to a specified group of people are dissolved. My neighbor is the one who needs my help, whether he belongs to my nation or not, whether he is my friend or my enemy. Because God's love knows no boundary, the love for the neighbor is not permitted to stop at any border, even those borders where hate and hostility separate people from each other. That is why Jesus taught, "Love your enemies and pray for those who persecute you, so that you may be children of your Father who is in heaven; for he makes his sun rise on the evil and on the good, and sends rain on the just and on the unjust" (Matt. 5:44–45*).

PRAYER

In Jesus' age every Jew prayed three times a day, in the morning, at noon, and in the evening. For the most part, people made use of liturgically formed prayers, but one could also lift up one's needs to the God of Israel in one's own words. For example, one ancient Jewish prayer reflects this belief and practice:

Blessed and holy be his name in all the world, which he has created according to his will. May he let his kingdom come and his redemption spring forth during your lifetime and the life of the whole house of Israel, soon, in the near future. And let all say Amen! May his great name be praised forever. Blessed, praised, glorified, exalted, magnified, honored, lifted up, and extolled be his holy name. Praised be he in heaven by all hymns, songs, praises, and words of trust which are spoken in the world. And let all say Amen! May great peace come from heaven and may life come to us and to all Israel. And let all say, Amen!

In one of his parables Jesus tells how some people in his time prayed in the Temple (Luke 18:9–14). One was a Pharisee, the other a tax collector. The Pharisee stood up and prayed: "God, I thank thee that I am not like other men, extortioners, unjust, adulterers, or even like this tax collector." The Pharisee belonged to the association of religious people who had solemnly obligated themselves not to steal, not to lie, and to honor marriage. They kept their distance from the pagan occupation forces, and thereby also avoided contact with tax collectors as well. The Romans usually farmed out the tax contracts to those who offered the highest bid. Of course, there were officially set rates according to which customs and tariffs were supposed to be paid. But the tax collectors were clever about overcharging and pocketing the surplus themselves. Thus they were universally considered to be cheats. They could not be called as witnesses before Jewish courts, because no one believed them. Therefore, religious people kept their distance from them.

The Pharisee could point to the fact that he was willing to let his faith cost him something, and even went beyond the prescriptions set forth by the Old Testament: "I fast twice a week, I give tithes of all that I get." To be sure, the Old Testament does prescribe that a tenth of one's income be given for the support of the priestly ministry in the temple (Deut. 14:22–29). This commandment, however, was not taken very seriously by most people. People attempted to evade it whenever it was possible. The Pharisees opposed such conduct and painstakingly paid attention to the exact requirement of tithing everything. The Old Testament speaks of fasting only in connection with the great Day of Atonement which was observed once a year for the expiation of Israel's sins (Lev. 16:29–34). The Pharisees, however, voluntarily fasted twice a week, on Monday and Thursday. That means that they not only ate nothing from early morning until late evening but also that despite the hot climate they drank nothing either. By this means they wanted to grant God the honor due him.

The Pharisees led a life pleasing to God and were respected by people. The words of the prayer quoted by Jesus in the parable are thoroughly consistent with the prayers spoken by the pious of that time. Thus a prayer from the first century A.D., preserved in the Talmud, reads as follows: "I thank you Lord my God, that you have given me my part among those who sit in the house of study rather than those who sit on the street corners; for I get up early, and they get up early: I get up early to study the words of the Law, and they get up early for worthless things. I work hard, and they work hard: I work hard and receive a reward, they work hard and receive no reward. I run, and they run: I run toward the life of the future world, and they run toward the grave of corruption." "I thank you"—the prayer of this righteous man contains only thanksgiving. But with these words he marks himself off from those whose lives have not turned out so well as has his, or who have never even tried to do God's will. Therefore, with a high sense of pride he looks down on the tax collector who also stands in the temple, and prays, "I thank you, God, that I am not like this tax collector."

The tax collector, however, does not even dare to lift up his eyes to heaven. He bursts out with a desperate cry, "God, be merciful to me a sinner." No additional word, only this cry. He beats his breast so as to express grief. For how could he ever be restored to a right relation to God? According to the views of that time, he must correct the wrong which he has done. But he can no longer even determine the identity of the many people he has cheated. And since, according to the prevailing doctrine, God's forgiveness can be granted only to those who make compensation to those against whom they have done wrong, the tax collector remains excluded from God's grace. He knows that he is lost. His only hope is directed to God alone. God might do what seems impossible to the religious people: be merciful. "This man went down to his house justified rather than the other," concludes the parable (Luke 18:14). Jesus thereby rejects the prayer of the pious and accepts that of the tax collector. The tax collector had accepted God's judgment as just, but the Pharisee thought he was able to declare God's judgment himself. God accepts the lost, but rejects the proud.

How should one pray? "Lord, teach us to pray"—with this request the disciples turn to Jesus (Luke 11:1). They had known from childhood that people were supposed to pray to God. But they wanted to learn from Jesus the true nature of prayer. Do not use many extra words, said Jesus; do not chatter on and on like the heathen. Do not choose a spot for your prayer where a lot of people will see you. "But when you pray, go into your room and shut the door and pray to your Father who is in secret; and your Father who sees in secret will reward you" (Matt. 6:6–7). The simple house in which a family in ancient Palestine lived usually consisted of only one room in which the family lived by day and slept at night. The only place which was enclosed was the small food pantry or "closet." When one wants to pray to God, one should seek out such a private place. There is no need to visit a special holy place in order to spend a few minutes of quiet meditation. Nor does one need many words. ''For your Father knows what you need before you ask him'' (Matt. 6:8). Prayer is an expression of trust in God. In prayer one honestly lifts up both anxieties and joys to God, the one who knows what is good for us. Therefore, ''Pray then like this.''

> Father,
> Hallowed be thy name.
> Thy kingdom come.
> Give us each day our daily bread.
> And forgive us our sins;
> for we ourselves forgive each one
> who is indebted to us.
> And lead us not into temptation (Luke 11:2–4*).

This version of ''the Lord's Prayer'' which appears in the Gospel of Luke is shorter than the usual form with which we are familiar—the parallel in Matt. 6:9–13. Of course, later manuscripts also supplemented Luke's version by adding the third petition (''Thy will be done on earth as it is in heaven'') and the seventh (''but deliver us from evil''), as well as adding the closing doxology. But the oldest manuscripts of the Gospel of Luke contain only this terse prayer. The prayer was obviously ''handed on'' in the oral traditions of early Christianity in a shorter *and* a longer form. This shows that the prayer taught by Jesus was not understood as a rigidly fixed form; rather it offered an outline which could be filled out and expanded. As a guide for prayer, the Lord's Prayer points to those aspects of praying on which everything depends.

In the address with which the worshiper turns to God, he is not called upon as Lord and King, nor as Creator and Ruler of the universe, but as ''our Father.'' We may approach God in the same way that small children, with complete trust, approach their own fathers. Brevity of expression and joyful confidence are thus characteristic of the few sentences of the prayer which Jesus gives his disciples. God's name deserves honor; may it be kept holy. Everything which pertains to God is holy, whose name should not be abused for purposes of magic or for securing one's own gain.

God will finally reveal that he is holy and that he rules. Thus the prayer "Thy kingdom come!" means "Let your glory become visible and your majesty be acknowledged. And now quickly reveal your glory, and do not delay to fulfill what you have promised," as expressed in a contemporary prayer. God's kingdom will bring all evil activity to an end and establish righteousness, which will be seen as God's mercy.

Just as the first part of the Lord's Prayer is oriented toward God ("thy")—concerned with God's name and his kingdom—so the second part speaks of us ("our") and what we need for our life. "Daily bread" is required for each day. "O Lord our God, bless this year that it might be a fruitful one in every way. Give the land dew and rain, fill the earth from the treasures of your goodness. Praised be thou, O Lord, who blesses the year." So people prayed in the synagogue. Jesus fully expressed this same prayer in his extremely brief request—"Give us each day our daily bread." Whoever prays to God with such trust will enter into the tough work which still must be done every day without anxiety. For such a person is confident that God will supply each day's need.

In addition to daily bread there is another gift which is no less important. The "and" connects it closely with the preceding request, "And forgive us our sins." People in the ancient world were thoroughly aware of the meaning of this prayer. "Our Father, our King, forgive and excuse all our sins, blot out our transgressions and remove them far from your eyes. Our Father, our King, according to your great mercy cancel all our debts"—so an ancient Jewish prayer implored God. Again, the Lord's Prayer says the same thing with utmost brevity. God will remove the separation which we have caused by our sinful conduct. He alone can take away what we wish had never happened. He hears the prayer of the one who calls to him, "God, be merciful to me a sinner." That is why the prayer continues, "And lead us not into temptation." "Temptation" refers to events which could take us away from God and destroy our fellowship with him. If God remains near us, then we are cared for, and nothing can separate us from him.

In the ancient world, every prayer ended with a doxology. Usually, however, the worshiper expressed this in his or her own words. This is why the oldest tradition of the Lord's Prayer contains no formal conclusion. Very soon, however, a liturgical form was composed which was then also taken up in the written text of the prayer: "For thine is the kingdom and the power and the glory forever. Amen." The "amen" means "so be it." Whoever says "amen" expresses: "That should really happen!" God knows what we need. That is why the prayer is permeated with joy. But the worshipers also know what the prayer requires of them: ". . . for we ourselves forgive every one who is indebted to us."

MIRACLES

Jesus not only spoke with an incomparable authority, which called forth both astonishment and admiration from his audiences, but he also performed deeds about which people said: "We have never seen anything like this." All four evangelists report such mighty works or miracles.

Thus Mark reports that when Jesus taught in the synagogue at Capernaum everyone was deeply impressed by the power of his teaching. Suddenly, a man possessed with an unclean (i.e., evil) spirit stood up and cried out, "What do you want from us, Jesus of Nazareth? You have come to destroy us! I know who you are, the Holy One of God!" In the ancient world it was believed that if one knew the name of another, he could exercise power over him. That is why the evil spirit who had possessed the man addressed Jesus by name. He thought that in this way he could defend himself against Jesus and avoid being driven out of his victim. But Jesus—so the story continues—spoke to him with sovereign authority: "Be silent, and come out of him!" The result was immediately apparent. The evil spirit convulsed the sick man, throwing him wildly about, and then with a loud scream came out of him. Jesus was more powerful than the demon: he defeated it. All those who were present were amazed, and asked each other, "What is this? A new teaching with authority!" (Mark 1:21–28*).

In the communities of Jesus and the first Christians people were well acquainted with stories of amazing healings of those who had been sick. For instance, let us compare the story of Mark 1:21–28 with a similar story from those times, one which also tells the story of a demon-possessed person who was healed. The philosopher Apollonius of Tyana was a wandering teacher of the first century A.D. who in the course of his travels once appeared in Athens. In the audience there was a young man who led a notoriously wicked life. As he listened to the discourse of the philosopher, he broke out in loud, shameless laughter. Then Apollonius looked intently at him and said, "It is not you who are conducting yourself so outrageously here, but the evil spirit by which you are possessed!" The struggle between this evil spirit and the miracle worker is then portrayed in the following words:

> He was, however—so they said—really possessed, but people had not realized it. He laughed when no one else laughed, cried for no reason, sang and talked to himself. People thought this was just the result of his licentious life. But an evil demon had possessed him, and when he was acting so outrageously he appeared to be drunk. Now when Apollonius continued to look at him intently with growing anger, the demon cried out like one under a curse or one who was being tortured on the rack, and swore to leave the young man alone and never to enter another person again. But as Apollonius spoke to him like an angry master to a shameless evil slave, and commanded him both to leave the youth and to give some visible sign that he had come out, the demon cried out, "I will overturn that statue there"— and pointed to a sculpture in the royal hall. The statue then really did begin to move, and fell to the floor. What fear! What amazement! Who could describe it? The young man, however, rubbed his eyes as if awaking from sleep, looked at the rays of the sun, and was embarrassed because all eyes were fixed on him. From then on he did not appear to be so wild and disorderly, but his healthy nature reappeared just as if he had taken some good medicine.

This narrative illustrates the *typical* characteristics of a miracle story, the story of someone's terrible sickness and its cure. The peculiar conduct of the young man is due to the activity of demons; they invade the lives of human beings. Spirits with superhuman powers may influence human beings positively and keep them in a good mood. But countless other evil spirits only want to harm people and enslave them. Only a limited number of folks have that extraordinary insight and saving gift of power necessary to drive them out. The intensity of the struggle with the powers of darkness is indicated by the description of the terrible sickness and the

helplessness of people who confront it. Against this dark background the event of an unexpected healing shines all the brighter.
The success of the healing is made apparent to everyone: the
demon overturns the statue on his way out and the young man who
has been freed from the demon now stands healthy before them—
cured.

The New Testament miracle stories embrace these characteristics which are typical of the miracle stories of the ancient world:
the portrayal of the sickness, the manner in which it is evaluated,
the healing by powerful words of an especially gifted person, and
the unprecedented effect of the event. The unique element in New
Testament miracle stories, however, is not the amazing event as
such, but the person of Jesus who stands at the center of the
story—told with considerably more brevity than the pagan stories.
Jesus is Lord—that is their essential message. His words are filled
with unique power, able to overcome sickness and suffering. The
question "Who is this?" is answered by the evangelists: "Jesus,
the Holy One of God." On the one hand, these early Christian
miracle stories do exhibit features which are common in the comparable stories of the ancient world. On the other hand, such
comparisons make their special character all the more apparent.
They want to preach Jesus Christ, the one who testifies to the
presence of God not only with his words but with his deeds. The
deeds of Jesus touch the lives of people—with renewing power—
and let them experience the transforming power of his word.

Jesus is Lord not only over evil spirits and sickness but also over
the powers of nature. This message is set forth in stories which
emphasize his incomparable sovereignty. In the late evening of a
long day, so the Gospel of Mark reports, Jesus got into a boat with
his disciples in order to cross to the other side of the lake of
Gennesaret. A storm suddenly descended on the lake. Waves were
breaking into the boat, filling it up, and Jesus was lying asleep on a
cushion in the stern of the boat. The disciples woke him up and said
to him, "Teacher, do you not care if we perish?" But Jesus stood
up, rebuked the wind, and spoke to the sea, "Silence! Be still!"
The wind ceased, and there was a great calm. Then Jesus said to
them, "Why are you so afraid? Have you no faith?" But they were

very afraid and said to one another, "Who is this? Even the wind and the sea obey him!" (Mark 4:35–41*).

Other stories from that time also tell of how a storm suddenly ended and a ship in distress had been saved. For instance, a story from the Jewish tradition tells how a ship was once seized by a violent storm. All the people on board cried to the various gods they each worshiped. But they cried in vain; all the praying did not help. A small Jewish child also happened to be on board. People advised him that he should also cry out to his god. As he prayed to the God of Israel for help, the storm suddenly stopped, and the ship arrived at its destination without damage. This story is told in order to praise the power of prayer when a pious Israelite prays. The New Testament story, on the other hand, declares that Jesus himself has the power through his word to put the wind and the sea in their place.

The authority of Jesus Christ is also the subject of those stories in which he calls back to life someone who has just died. He steps into a situation where the daughter of an official of the synagogue had become sick and died. He grasped the child by the hand and spoke, "Talitha cumi," which means "Little girl, I say to you, arise." Immediately the girl got up and walked, and the crowds were overcome with amazement (Mark 5:35–43). According to the Gospel of Luke, Jesus once met a funeral procession in which the only son of a widow was being carried to his grave. He touched the coffin and said to the dead man, "Young man, I say to you, arise." Immediately the dead man sat up and began to speak, and Jesus gave him to his mother (Luke 7:11–17). Although a story of someone being raised from the dead may be unheard of in our times, nevertheless here is another instance where the ancient world was familiar with comparable stories. The Old Testament tells how the prophet Elijah stretched himself out over the body of the dead child of the widow of Zarephath and cried out to God, "O Lord my God, let this child's life come back into him" (1 Kings 17:21*). The prayer of Elijah was heard, and life returned to the child. A similar story is told of Elisha: he stretched himself out over a dead child until its body became warm and it was restored to life (2 Kings 4:34). Just by telling of the return of someone from the dead does not as such make a story unique; rather the New Testament stories are concerned to show who Jesus is. He wins the victory over death through his mighty word and gives new life.

While stories were told of people with extraordinary powers, both before and during Jesus' time, the Gospels are completely directed toward the person of Jesus—*the center of the gospel message*. He is the bearer of good news. Luke speaks of him as the one who makes the poor rich and fills the hands of the empty. Thus the message which the evangelists want to communicate by means of the miracle stories would be misunderstood if one was interested in investigating whether all these events really happened exactly as they are told. There can be no doubt that Jesus performed extraordinary deeds. The reports that tell of these deeds have just as surely added much to them, and also made use of the means of expression which were used in the miracle stories of the ancient world.

The significance of the miracle stories, in the context of their proclamation about Christ himself, is clarified by the answer which Jesus gave to the query of John the Baptist. As John sat in prison he heard of Jesus' deeds. John came to fully doubt and question whether Jesus really was the one who was to come, or whether we must wait for another. In order to be certain about this, he sent two of his disciples to Jesus to put this question directly to him. Jesus answered, "Go and tell John what you hear and see: the blind receive their sight and the lame walk, lepers are cleansed and the deaf hear, and the dead are raised up, and the poor have good news preached to them" (Matt. 11:4–5). These words take up the prophetic promises. They speak of the promise that in the time of salvation the deaf will hear and the eyes of the blind will see, the needy will again rejoice in the Lord, and the poorest people will be happy (Isa. 29:18–19). Then the lame shall leap like a deer, and the tongue of the dumb will sing for joy (Isa. 35:5–6). Jesus answered the messengers from John: what the prophets have promised is now being fulfilled. Even the dead are being brought back to life. But even that is not the greatest of all miracles. The most wonderful one stands at the end of this story: "And the poor have good news preached to them."

THE SERMON ON THE MOUNT

"Seeing the crowds, he went up on the mountain, and when he sat down his disciples came to him. And he opened his mouth and taught them, saying . . ." (Matt. 5:1–2). With these words Matthew introduces the major speech of Jesus, usually called the Sermon on the Mount. Just as Moses once ascended Mount Sinai and there received the commandments from God which he delivered to the people of Israel, so now Jesus takes his disciples up on a mountain and declares to them how they should live and conduct themselves amidst the signs of the dawning kingdom of God. Their righteousness must surpass that of the scribes and the Pharisees (Matt. 5:20). This is not to suggest that in the Judaism of that time there were no sincere religious people who with great earnestness attempted to live a life pleasing to God. Nor does the emphasis lie upon efforts to outdo the scribes and Pharisees by achieving even greater accomplishments. On the contrary, it is a matter of realizing that the new righteousness is the way of discipleship into which Jesus' disciples are called. The Sermon on the Mount illustrates what that means by concrete examples.

The Sermon on the Mount begins with a series of *Beatitudes* (Matt. 5:3–12). These verses are significant because they determine the direction for the whole speech. They show that the new righteousness which the disciples of Jesus are to live out receives its power from the gift of the divine grace which is granted to the poor, sorrowing, meek, hungering, and thirsting people of this world. Each of these affirmations is followed by a statement on which it is based. The first and last of these are identical: "for theirs is the kingdom of heaven" (Matt. 5:3, 10). They receive the promise that they will participate in the future salvation. On the basis of this promise, however, they are already pronounced blessed. Thus the Beatitudes are intended to point out the conditions under which entrance to the coming kingdom of God may be granted: not on the basis of extraordinary accomplishment or worthy deeds, but exclusively by virtue of that trusting devotion by which the poor and persecuted, the sorrowing, and the peacemakers are graciously accepted by God. The final clauses are consistently expressed in

the future tense: "they will be comforted," "they will be satisfied," "they will receive mercy." The cautious manner of expression, to avoid directly pronouncing the name of God, is intended to say that God will act for them: he will comfort them, he
will satisfy them, he will show mercy to them. The Beatitudes
thereby point to the glory of the coming kingdom of God, the
anticipatory signs of which are already to be seen in that the poor,
the hungry, the sorrowing, and the merciful are already pronounced blessed. They are the ones who are conscious that they
stand before God with empty hands. But God wants to fill them.

The first four Beatitudes speak of people who in their particular
kind of need set their hope on God: the poor, the sorrowful, the
hungering, and thirsting. The second part of the series names
people who are pronounced blessed on the basis of a certain kind of
conduct. Then a final sentence is appended which spills over into a
direct address to the disciples: "Blessed are you when men revile
you and persecute you and utter all kinds of evil against you falsely
on my account" (Matt. 5:11). In their sufferings the disciples of
Jesus share the destiny of the rejected prophet, and they become
aware of what it means that they are called to function as the salt of
the earth and the light of the world (Matt. 5:13–16).

If one reads straight through the three chapters of the Sermon on
the Mount (Matthew 5—7), one quickly gets the impression that it
is not reporting an actual speech which was given all at the same
time. Thus in chapter 7, for example, one saying is joined to
another without any recognizable continuity in the thought:
"Judge not, that you be not judged" (7:1). "Do not give dogs what
is holy" (7:6). "Ask, and it will be given you" (7:7). "So whatever
you wish that men would do to you, do so to them" (7:12). The
whole unit is obviously formed from individual sayings, which
were only later combined into a larger composition. This insight is
confirmed when one places the parallel section of Luke 6:20–49
beside Matthew 5—7 for comparison. There a shorter speech by
Jesus is reported, usually called the "Sermon on the Plain," because there Jesus stood on a "level place" while he addressed the
disciples and the people (Luke 6:17). Like the Sermon on the
Mount, the Sermon on the Plain begins with beatitudes, only four,

which are then followed by four corresponding woes. To this material the sayings about love for enemies are joined, paralleled in Matt. 5:39–48. Next come sayings which speak of mercy and the attitude one should have to the neighbor, as in Matt. 7:1–5, then the section about good and bad trees (cf. Matt. 12:33–35). Like the Sermon on the Mount, the Sermon on the Plain concludes by comparing those who hear Jesus' words and do them to a man who built his house on a solid rock (Luke 6:47–49//Matt. 7:24–27). The beginning and end of both speeches are quite similar. Almost every item found in the Sermon on the Plain is also found in the Sermon on the Mount. But beyond that, the Sermon on the Mount contains material which is located elsewhere in the Gospel of Luke: thus the Lord's Prayer (Matt. 6:9–13//Luke 11:1–4), the sayings about anxiety (Matt. 6:24–33//Luke 12:22–33), or the image of the wide and narrow gates (Matt. 7:13–14//Luke 13:23–24). Reflection on this comparison leads to a clear conclusion: the Sermon on the Plain as found in the Gospel of Luke represents the outline of an originally much shorter speech which must also have been among the sources used by the evangelist Matthew. He used it as the framework into which he inserted numerous words and sayings of Jesus known to him from the oral tradition. In this way he constructed his extensive composition known as the Sermon on the Mount, his programmatic summary of the preaching of Jesus.

How Jesus' disciples are to live according to God's will is elaborated in six *antitheses,* structured in accordance with a fixed formal schema (Matt. 5:21–48). Each of them begins with a reference to Scripture and tradition known from the past: "You have heard. . . ." The ancient rule is then juxtaposed to Jesus' authoritative word: "But I say to you." Then in each case the argument is developed that God's will is violated not just with the transgression of the well-known commandments, but already by an evil word or malicious thought. Not only through a physical attack on a person's life, but already by an angry outburst the command "Thou shalt not kill" is broken. And not only through physical adultery is God's command broken, but already the man who lustfully looks at the wife of another disdains God's will. Over against the iron rule, "an eye for an eye, a tooth for a tooth," Jesus places: "But I say to you, Do not resist one who is evil. But if any one strikes you on the right cheek, turn to him the other also; and if any one would sue you and take your coat, let him have your cloak as well" (Matt. 5:39–40).

Can people really live this way? Is any one at all able to live by such strict commands? These questions have been discussed since biblical times. It has been thought that the Sermon on the Mount was intended to serve as a mirror which reflects our own inadequacy, in order to make it clear to all who look into it that they stand guilty before God and are lost without his grace. However valuable such a line of thought may be, it hardly corresponds with the intention which the evangelist detected in the preaching of Jesus, when at the end of the Sermon he speaks of "every one who hears my words and does them" (7:24*). Accordingly, the Sermon on the Mount is intended to give practical instructions for actual living. But are its demands perhaps so high that no one can satisfy them?

If one will understand the meaning of the demands in the Sermon on the Mount, one must not lose sight of the way it begins. It is not rules and regulations that stand at the beginning, but the Beatitudes, the pronouncement of divine mercy. But the love of God referred to by the Sermon on the Mount is an attack on the world as we conceive it to be. God's love does not want to confirm the existing order of the world but to renew it from the ground up. Thus the Sermon on the Mount contains no ready-made program for the reform of the world or for the organization of social relationships, but it beckons people to hear Jesus' word, to trust it, and to do it. Therefore, this sermon cannot be understood apart from its preacher, apart from Jesus Christ. But Jesus does not want from us this or that work, however great a sacrifice it may represent; he wants us, our very selves. Again and again this is expressed in the antitheses in the form "you have heard it said—but I say to you," in order to show by each example that at no point in our life can we find a spot where the will and sovereignty of God does not apply. *We are responsible at every point.* Therefore, Jesus chooses examples which are formulated in a radical way so as to forbid a lustful look or any form of revenge. These words would be misunderstood, however, if one were to think: if I always turn back the other cheek when I am struck, then God's will is really fulfilled. Even this thinking would not grasp the meaning of Jesus' teaching. He does not want this or that work, but us, with all that we have and are. The apostle Paul says that without love, even the most magnificent deeds of renunciation and surrender mean nothing at all (1 Cor. 13:1–3).

The Sermon on the Mount, then, does not intend to force us to strive for unattainable moral accomplishments, but intends to show us that we belong totally to God, and that we can and should live from the power of his grace. For where our treasure is, there our heart will be also (Matt. 6:21). In what do we place our trust? Only if the joyful pronouncement of blessing, with which the Sermon on the Mount begins, receives first place will its call to repentance be rightly understood. Salvation is pronounced to those who stand before God as recipients of a gift. But this very pronouncement gives them the basis for a new life.

The first hearers of Jesus' preaching obviously perceived that his words gripped people and that he spoke with incomparable power. In this vein Matthew concludes the Sermon on the Mount with the observation that people were astonished at his teaching: "For he taught them as one who had authority, and not as their scribes" (Matt. 7:28–29).

FOR FURTHER READING

Bonhoeffer, Dietrich. *The Cost of Discipleship*. New York: Macmillan Co., 1967.

Brown, Raymond E. "The Gospel Miracles." In *The Jerome Biblical Commentary*, pp. 784–88. Edited by Raymond E. Brown, Joseph A. Fitzmeyer, and Roland E. Murphy. Englewood Cliffs, N.J.: Prentice-Hall, 1968.

Crossan, John Dominic. *In Parables: The Challenge of the Historical Jesus*. New York: Harper & Row, 1973.

Ebeling, Gerhard. *On Prayer: The Lord's Prayer in Today's World*. Philadelphia: Fortress Press, 1978.

Hunter, A. M. *The Parables Then and Now*. Philadelphia: Westminster Press, 1972.

Interpreter's Dictionary of the Bible, 1962 ed. Entry of "Miracle," by S. V. McCasland.

Jeremias, Joachim. *The Lord's Prayer*. Philadelphia: Fortress Press, Facet Books, 1964.

——. *Rediscovering the Parables*. New York: Charles Scribner's Sons, 1966.

——. *The Sermon on the Mount*. Philadelphia: Fortress Press, Facet Books, 1963.

Küng, Hans. *On Being a Christian*. New York: Doubleday & Co., 1976.

3

FAITH AND THE FAITHFUL COMMUNITY

The Beginnings of the Christian Church

CHRISTIANS

At first the followers of Jesus of Nazareth were regarded as a group which had developed within Judaism, especially characterized by its faith: the Messiah had come. They were thereby placed in the same category as other religious associations which had gained a group identity in first-century Judaism. The gospels and Acts frequently mention the Sadducees and the Pharisees; other groups, not referred to by the writings of the New Testament, are named and described in the Jewish literature of that time.

The name *Sadducee* is certainly related to the name *Zadok,* a High Priest in the days of King Solomon (1 Kings 2:35). As members of the priestly family they lived in Jerusalem where they had organized themselves into an aristocratic association. On the one hand they were committed to carrying out a careful political policy, under the Roman rule, which clearly renounced all revolutionary aspirations. On the other hand, as priests and guardians of the tradition, they were concerned to hold strictly to the letter of the Law from the Old Testament, and were concerned that it be carried out in practice. Their conservative, prosaic thought had no room for the later doctrines of angels and demons. And above all, they rejected the idea that the dead would be raised at the Last Day (Acts 23:8), for they could find no basis at all for this doctrine in the five books of Moses (Genesis—Deuteronomy). By being politically circumspect and by clever dealing they were able to occupy the respected offices in Jerusalem, even during the rule of King Herod and the Roman governors. The High Priests, who installed the current rulers in their offices, always came from the circles of the Sadducees.

The *Pharisees* were clearly distinguished from the Sadducees not only on the basis of their organization but also their doctrine. Their name means literally "the separated ones," a label probably first given them by outsiders, for as the holy community of God they sought to avoid contact with all that was unclean. By a pious life, fasting, and prayer they wanted to prepare themselves for the great future transformation which God would bring about. They were intent on seeing to it that the laws of purity listed in the Law (Torah) were conscientiously followed. For example, whoever touched a corpse or dead animal had lost the state of cultic cleanliness. In order to be restored to it, one must take a ritual bath of purification. Before every meal the Pharisees washed their hands (Mark 7:3–4), in order to be able to lift up pure hands in prayer. They were concerned, however, not only with the ritual purity of people but also with the utensils which they used. Pharisees gave a tithe to the temple, not only of the produce of their own lands but also of everything which they purchased. They even tithed spices and herbs (Matt. 23:23//Luke 11:42). Over and above these things which were prescribed, they voluntarily took on additional religious obligations, such as fasting (Luke 18:12) or acts of charity by which they sought to help the poor or those in distress.

The associations of Pharisees included some priests, but mostly laymen: craftsmen, farmers, businessmen, who lived not only in Jerusalem but also in the countryside of Galilee and Judea. They gathered together for common meals, because they could then keep the laws of purity all the better (Luke 7:36; 11:37–38). According to their teaching, the oral tradition held equal value alongside the written word of the Law (Torah). By means of the ingenious interpretations which oral tradition contained they sought to adapt the divine command so comprehensively to the present that one could find practical regulations for every aspect of life—for example, instructions concerning precisely how the Sabbath was to be kept. In this regard their interpretations were more liberal and progressive than those of the Sadducees, who interpreted strictly according to the letter of the Law. In an emergency where life was in danger, the Pharisaic view allowed exceptions to help people who had fallen into misfortune, without violating God's will in the matter. The tradition of the elders (Mark 7:3), that is, the tradition elaborated and transmitted by the scribes, to which they held fast, had developed the expectation of the resurrection of the dead into a firmly formulated doctrine (Acts 23:8). According to their hopes, if the people would prepare themselves in purity and holiness for the coming of the Messiah, then the Son of David would appear to gather the scattered tribes of Israel together and reestablish the kingdom.

A third group, greatly admired because of its strict adherence to the Law and its pious manner of life, is not mentioned in the New Testament. It is known in some detail from contemporary reports and from recently found documents. They too probably received their name from outsiders. They were called *Essenes,* that is, "the Pious." Their understanding of the Law and their manner of life are described in the Dead Sea Scrolls, discovered in caves on the west bank of the Dead Sea some thirty-five years ago. There these Essenes inhabited a monasterylike community at Qumran; it must have been the center of all the groups which belonged to this association. It was destroyed in A.D. 68, in the war in which the Romans put an end to the Jewish revolt throughout the country. As the Roman troops approached, these devout Jews securely hid their sacred writings so that they could recover them later. But apparently none of these Jews survived the war, so the sacred scrolls did not see the light of day again until our own time (1947).

In loyalty to the Law, Essenes gathered together in the wilderness, wanting to be obedient to the covenant of Israel, to turn away from the world of godlessness and lies, and to return to the law of Moses. They studied the biblical writings, because they found in them the destiny of "the pious" already described in advance, namely that they would be rejected and persecuted by the ruling priesthood in Jerusalem. Since they believed they stood over against a world of darkness and lies, they saw it as their duty to equip God's combat squad for battle. The Sons of Light must do battle with the Sons of Darkness. The time in which the community found itself was a time of purification and testing, in which the spirits were divided: truth and lie, light and darkness went their separate ways. At the same time, this division made visible on which side God had placed each individual person and determined his or her lot. All who belonged to the community of salvation were in need of constant discipline and testing. Just as the priests had to be intent on preserving cultic purity, so every member of the Qumran community had to carry out daily the prescribed ritual washings. Only as one who is ritually clean could one with a repentant heart belong to the community and participate in the common meals, with a priest presiding. In order to safeguard this ritual purity, the members of the covenant community apparently renounced marriage and family. After a long probationary period, those who were finally accepted handed over their personal property to the community; it was added to the community of goods and from then on belonged to all.

And so the community of the covenant kept itself constantly ready for the imminent triumph of God, who would manifest his victory over all evil powers in the near future. According to their expectation, God would send to his people a prophet and two anointed ones, the Messiah of Aaron and the Messiah of Israel. Then the priestly and the secular rulers of the people of God would stand side by side as they led the redeemed community. Even so, first place was to be given to the messianic priest, because he would establish the purity of God's community and take away all its uncleanness.

In the eyes of many contemporaries, the followers of Jesus of Nazareth appeared to be just another group within Judaism. The Acts of the Apostles reports that it was in the great Syrian city of Antioch that the disciples of Jesus were for the first time called "Christians" (Acts 11:26). All who confessed the crucified and risen Jesus of Nazareth to be the Messiah thereby expressed that they belonged to Jesus as their Lord and wanted to follow him as his disciples. They did not describe themselves as "Christians," but were first so named by outsiders. People observed how they came together and listened to what they said. The central affirmation of their preaching was: Jesus is the Messiah, the anointed one of God. In Greek this message is expressed in the title "the Christ." In accordance with this content of their faith the name "Christian" was coined. The principal characteristic of being a

Christian is the confession of faith, "We belong to the Messiah, we are the people of the crucified and risen Messiah." Thus people called them "Messiah-people," "Christ-ians." But as it dawned upon people that they were talking about a Messiah who had already come, and, moreover, had suffered a shameful death on the cross, people began to perceive that there was a fundamental difference between the Christians and the other religious associations of the Judaism of that time.

CHURCH

The first Christians did not withdraw from the world, unlike the Jewish community at Qumran which established its center on the edge of the Dead Sea. Instead they gathered together in Jerusalem and Galilee, and soon also in the cities and towns of those countries situated in the Mediterranean world. They were aware of a responsibility they had to spread the message which did not just belong to an exclusive group, but to all people. They called themselves "the elect" (Rom. 8:33; 1 Pet. 1:1; and elsewhere), "the called" (Rom. 1:6; 1 Cor. 1:24; and elsewhere), and "the saints" (1 Cor. 6:2; 16:1; and elsewhere). All these designations were already found in the Old Testament, where they were applied to the people of God, Israel. God called his people (Hos. 11:1), he elected them (Ps. 105:43), and he sanctified them (Ps. 4:4; Isa. 62:12). This does not mean that God singled them out for special privileges above other people. Israel often disappointed her God, and was often disobedient. Rather, election, calling, and sanctification mean that God has made these people into his own people and considers them his own property. Election is therefore not the proof of some special excellence, but an expression of Israel's belonging to God, and of the obligation which goes with it. An object or an animal might be called holy ("sanctified")—withdrawn from common use and designated exclusively for use in the Temple or for a sacrifice there—because it belongs to God. "Holiness" is not a designation for especially good moral conduct. Rather, as God's chosen and called, it is a mark of those who have been led into his service.

The first Christians took up these designations from the Old Testament and applied them to themselves in order to show that they were the Israel of God (Gal. 6:16), the twelve tribes, and the ones brought together from the dispersion by God (James 1:1; 1 Pet. 1:1). When Israel was gathered together at Sinai to receive the Law, they heard the voice of God declare, "You shall be my own possession among all peoples . . . you shall be to me a kingdom of priests and a holy nation" (Exod. 19:5–6). In the New Testament these words are applied to the Christian community, "But you are a chosen race, a royal priesthood, a holy nation, God's own people, that you may declare the wondrous deeds of him who called you out of darkness into his marvelous light" (1 Pet. 2:9).

Among the different terms that the first Christians used to describe themselves, one was especially favored: *congregation* or *church*. These two terms, usually used in German, and often in English, express contrasting meanings and represent the same Greek word: *ekklēsia*—a word which was taken over without change into Latin and is still commonly used today (ecclesia). This usage has also been influenced by the previous history of the word in the Old Testament, where it is used for the "congregation of the Lord" (Deut. 23:2–4): those who had been drafted into God's holy army came together in order to march into the land promised to them and live there under God's commandment. It was God's call which created Israel as his people. Thus Israel only remains true to its destiny when it responds to this call. The first Christians understood themselves as this congregation of God and thus as the heirs of Israel to whom the promises of the Scriptures applied. God has remained true to his word and has honored the pledges which he has made to his people.

Wherever Christians call on the name of their Lord, there God's congregation is gathered. The New Testament can thus use the word *church* sometimes in the singular and sometimes in the plural without making a distinction between the two. Thus in his letter to the Galatians (Gal. 1:2) the apostle Paul first addresses *the churches* in Galatia (in Asia Minor). Then he mentions that as a Jew he had persecuted *the church of God* (Gal. 1:13). Finally he notes that after his conversion he was not known personally to the Christian *churches* in Judea (Gal. 1:22). From this usage of the word *church,* which changes from plural to singular and then back again to plural, it is clear that no conceptual distinction is being made between the church as a local congregation and the church composed of all Christians. The local congregation, wherever it may be gathered, is the people of God, and confesses the name of its God. That community of people called by God and set apart as his own possession is the church, and it proclaims God's glory.

What was the life of an early Christian church like? We have more detailed reports about the Corinthian church than any other early Christian congregation. The apostle Paul had founded the church and had been able to work there a year and a half (Acts 18:11). But when a new governor began his term in Corinth, some Jews charged the apostle with misleading the people, teaching them to worship God in a different way than that commanded in the Law (Acts 18:13). The conflicts which arose from this charge compelled Paul to leave the city and the new congregation. Since the term of the Roman governor began yearly in the provincial capital, and since the name of the new governor, Gallio, is also mentioned in other ancient documents, these events can be dated with some precision. From these data we can infer that Paul arrived in Corinth at the end of A.D. 49 or beginning of A.D. 50, and remained there until the late spring of 51. The church which originated from his missionary work contained people from different backgrounds, reflecting the population of the Greek harbor city: "Not many of you were wise according to worldly standards, not many were powerful, not many were of noble birth; but God chose what is foolish in the world, God chose what is weak and despised in the world" (1 Cor. 1:26–28*). Jews and Gentiles, Greeks and barbarians, slaves and free, men and women became Christians, who met as the congregation of God in the home of various members of the church who owned large houses. The apostle addressed them as "saints in Christ Jesus," as "called saints" (1 Cor. 1:2). But he is forced to state in the letter that he writes to them that a sorry state of affairs has developed in this church. Customary ways of living in the surrounding world, ways of life which they themselves had previously shared, have reappeared in the lives of some Christians. One of them had taken his stepmother as his wife (1 Cor. 5:1–13). Others visited prostitutes, with no pangs of conscience (1 Cor. 6:12–20). Some doubted that there would be a resurrection of the dead (1 Cor. 15:12–19) and advocated the view that the blessed kingdom of the end time had already arrived (1 Cor. 4:8).

An early Christian congregation was anything but an ideal church, as is clear from the illustrations in 1 Corinthians. The same sort of evil and malicious activities which exist among people in general were also present among the Christians. Paul gives us an unretouched picture of congregational life in Corinth. But he tells the Corinthians that it must not remain that way, for "neither the immoral, nor idolaters, nor adulterers, . . . nor thieves, nor the greedy, nor drunkards, nor revilers, nor robbers will inherit the kingdom of God. And such were some of you" (1 Cor. 6:9–11). But all that is past history and may not be allowed to return, for the same text continues, "You were washed, you were sanctified, you were justified in the name of the Lord Jesus Christ and in the Spirit of our God." Whoever has been baptized into Christ belongs to him and should now live his or her life in obedience to the Lord. Christ has paid an inexpressibly high price for us, when he went to the cross for us—this is Paul's declaration to the church (1 Cor. 6:20; 7:23). Now live in a way that is appropriate to this: "Glorify God in your body" (6:20), "Do not become slaves of men" (7:23).

The church is *the body of Christ,* according to Paul, and the Christians are its individual limbs and organs. Paul uses the imagery of the body and its members in order to make clear how the church should live (1 Cor. 12:12–27). A body is composed of feet, ears, eyes, and many other members. Each member must fulfill its function in its place. The foot cannot say that it would rather be a hand. The eye cannot change places with the ear. Rather, the whole body is well only when every part performs the job for which it is designed. If one part is sick, the whole body is sick. And if one member should declare that it has no need of the others, it would soon notice how urgently it is dependent on them. Precisely those parts of the body which appear to be the weakest and least important we find to be most necessary. In this same way, God has assigned every member of the church an important place in the body as a whole; he has overlooked none. But he has not given the same assignment to each. Therefore the members are reacting in the wrong way when they look with envy and resentment on the gifts and assignments which have been given to others, thereby overlooking the importance of the task which they themselves have to fulfill. One does wrong to another by looking on him or her with disdain, as though his or her abilities and potential were less than one's own. The apostle warns against every tendency toward arrogance and also against the underevaluation of one's own gifts: "God has appointed in the church first apostles, second prophets, third teachers," but also a great variety of gifts; through them one person can be of help to the other (1 Cor. 12:28–31).

BAPTISM

Early Christianity practiced baptism from the very beginning. When Paul became a Christian a few years after the death of Jesus, baptism was already assumed to be the usual practice. This is clear from later statements of the apostle: ". . . all of us who have been baptized into Christ Jesus . . ." (Rom. 6:3) and "For by one Spirit we were all baptized into one body . . ." (1 Cor. 12:13). How did this early Christian practice of baptism originate?

In the environment of the New Testament, the view was widely prevalent that people could be contaminated by all sorts of cultic impurity; it had to be removed by ritual washings. Only a pure person may approach God. The Jewish community at Qumran— on the shore of the Dead Sea—was especially careful about this matter, insisting that the specifications for priestly purity given in the Law be kept by all the members of its community. Ritual washings were practiced every day. Only those who were in a state of ritual purity were permitted to participate in the meetings and common meals. But the effect of the ritual bath was not thought to take place merely by exact compliance with the rules for purity. In addition, one must have a repentant attitude in which all evil works are renounced and a commitment to total obedience to the Law is made.

On the banks of the Jordan, not far from the Dead Sea, appeared John the Baptist. He proclaimed that the wrath of God was about to be revealed in the final judgment (Matt. 3:7–10//Luke 3:7–9). John appealed to people to turn from the false way and prepare for the advent of *the one to come*. Great crowds came out to hear him and were moved by his preaching. They confessed their sins and were baptized by John. This baptism was described as precisely a "baptism of repentance" (Mark 1:4). In it, the renunciation of the false way found visible expression. In distinction from the daily washings practiced by the Qumran sect, so strictly oriented to keeping the Law, John's baptism was performed only once. Whoever has been baptized now belongs to the community of those who are prepared for the near advent of God and who will be saved in the coming judgment.

Among the crowds of people who came to John to be baptized by him, Jesus of Nazareth also was found (Mark 1:9). Why did he choose to number himself among that group who were confessing their sins? Would it not have been more appropriate for John to have been baptized *by* Jesus, instead of John baptizing Jesus? The answer is given, "in order to fulfill all righteousness" (Matt. 3:15). This means that at the very beginning of his ministry, Jesus associates himself with sinners, those to whom he wants to make the nearness of God's grace real.

The first Christians who came together after Good Friday and Easter continued to practice baptism as it had been done by John, but filled it with new meaning. The way in which the first Christian communities understood baptism is revealed in a text from an early Christian sermon: "Repent, and be baptized every one of you in the name of Jesus Christ for the forgiveness of your sins; and you shall receive the gift of the Holy Spirit" (Acts 2:38). Repentance, baptism, and the forgiveness of sins were also combined in the preaching of John the Baptist. But Christian baptism is distinctive in moving beyond John's, because it is performed in the name of Jesus Christ and because the gift of the Holy Spirit is received. The name of the Lord, to whom one now belongs, is pronounced over the one being baptized. This represents a change of lordships that will henceforth determine the person's whole life. He or she no longer belongs to those powers which had previously provided the norms for life, for Christ is now the Lord. The power of the Holy Spirit is experienced in the person's life as a guiding influence, meaning that God really is experienced as present and active. The baptized believer is convinced that he or she no longer lives out of his or her own resources, but has been granted the power of a new life. Thus the forgiveness of sins is no longer seen as a hoped-for future event, as in the preaching of John the Baptist; it is rather experienced as a present reality. This means that all who have been baptized into Christ are freed from the guilt of their past and are called to follow their Lord.

The Christian community knows that it has been authorized to baptize in the name of Jesus Christ by the Lord himself. It understands the command to baptize to come from the exalted Christ, who sends out his disciples into the world. They are commanded to preach the good news everywhere, and to baptize all who respond: "Go therefore and make disciples of all nations, baptizing them in the name of the Father and of the Son and of the Holy Spirit, teaching them to observe all that I have commanded you" (Matt. 28:19–20). So baptism, teaching, and faith belong together. This is why the church has always been engaged in explaining the significance of baptism, and has always given instruction about its significance to those who have wanted to be baptized. The Christian church is persuaded that God himself acts in the act of baptism. Therefore it is with good reason that it baptizes young children. The church also knows that it is obligated to explain to them later what it means to be a disciple of Jesus. For baptism only fulfills its power in those who in faith say their own "yes" to the gift they have received in it.

Whoever is baptized into Christ is thereby united with the death and resurrection of the Lord. In his letter to the church in Rome, the apostle Paul poses the question, "Do you not know that all of us who have been baptized into Christ Jesus were baptized into his death?" (Rom. 6:3). Paul here expressly speaks of that knowledge which is common to all Christians, and then adds: "We were buried therefore with him by baptism into death" (Rom. 6:4). Just as Christ was placed in the tomb after his death, so also the old self dies and is buried in baptism. The past is gone forever. A new life has begun under the sign of the resurrection of Jesus Christ.

What does that mean? Among some of the first Christians the view was advocated that in baptism the resurrection of the dead had already occurred (2 Tim. 2:18) and that the time of eternal blessedness had already arrived. We no longer need to be bothered with keeping God's commands, because we are already perfected in baptism, they thought. It is obvious, however, that such interpretations of baptism were already present in the apostle Paul's time, for he sets himself in the sharpest opposition to them. There can be no talk of the resurrection of the dead as something which is already present. We are baptized into the death of Christ—so Paul affirms—but the resurrection still lies in the future. For we are baptized into Christ's death, "so that as Christ was raised from the dead by the glory of the Father, we too might walk in newness of life" (Rom. 6:4). In contrast to a fanatically spiritualistic understanding of baptism—the voucher for our resurrection as something which has already happened and the presence of the divine power of salvation in our lives—Paul emphasizes that the old life has been done away with in baptism, but that the new life is to be lived in view of the future resurrection of the dead. Whoever disdains God's command can lose salvation and fall subject to God's judgment (1 Cor. 10:1–13). Thus the gift received in baptism can only be understood rightly when it is received *as the beginning* of discipleship to Christ.

Baptism places Christians in a new community in which the usual distinctions made by society are no longer valid. "For by one Spirit we were all baptized into one body—Jews or Greeks, slaves or free—and all were made to drink of one Spirit" (1 Cor. 12:13). And from this it follows: "There is neither Jew nor Greek, there is neither slave nor free, there is neither male nor female; for you are all one in Christ Jesus" (Gal. 3:28). Obviously Paul is aware that men and women continue to exist, that people continue to speak different languages, and that social distinctions which existed before baptism continue to exist afterwards. But they have lost their meaning in the Christian community and may no longer be permitted to separate people from each other. The new community in Christ includes all who have been baptized into him—members of his body.

THE LORD'S SUPPER

The first Christians regularly celebrated the Lord's Supper. People met in private homes, broke bread together, pronounced the blessing over it, and ate the meal together as they reflected on the death of Jesus Christ. The table fellowship which Jesus had with all sorts of people was thereby continued within the Christian congregations. Jesus had sat at the same table with those who were generally despised, with tax collectors and sinners, people with whom one was not supposed to have anything to do (cf. Mark 2:13–17; Luke 15:1–2; and elsewhere). Filled with indignation, the scribes and Pharisees had objected to this behavior, since to join in a common meal with others is to establish visible fellowship with them. People sat together at the same table not merely to eat, drink, and satisfy their physical appetites, but all those who sat around the table received a share in the divine blessing communicated through the words of prayer spoken over the food and drink: "Blessed art thou, King of the universe, who causest fruit to grow on the earth," or "Blessed art thou, O Lord, King of the universe, who dost create the fruit of the vine." The Jewish community at Qumran—on the banks of the Dead Sea—was very careful to allow only those who were ritually pure and who lived in accordance with the Law to participate in the common meal. Under the supervision of a priest, they came together to eat and drink new wine. The priest pronounced the blessing and thereafter everyone partook of the food and drink. But anyone who had not fulfilled the requirements of the Law was not permitted to participate.

How could Jesus sit at a table with people who obviously violated God's commands and paid no attention to what they meant for their lives? He answered that he had come to seek out the lost, and he did not hesitate to certify the gracious nearness of God for them. He shared food and drink with all who came to him. Sometimes great crowds streamed out after him in the open country. He served them, using just the available food: "And taking the five loaves and the two fish he looked up to heaven, and blessed, and broke the loaves, and gave them to the disciples to set before the people" (Mark 6:41). "And he took the seven loaves, and having given thanks he broke them and gave them to his disciples to set before the people" (Mark 8:6).

This table fellowship which Jesus had with the disciples and other people was continued by the first Christian communities.

"Breaking bread in their homes, they partook of food with glad and generous hearts" (Acts 2:46). After Good Friday and Easter, such meetings must have taken on a different character than the table fellowship during Jesus' lifetime. Immediately before his death Jesus gathered once again with his disciples and shared bread and wine with them. At that time he had told them that he would not drink the fruit of the vine with them again until that day in which they would drink it anew in the kingdom of God (Mark 14:25). In other words, Jesus and his disciples saw the coming great transformation of the kingdom of God as a near future reality. After Jesus' farewell the disciples found themselves alone, but they knew themselves to be united with the resurrected Lord and remained bound together in their confession to him in that fellowship which Jesus had founded.

The meaning of the celebration of the Lord's Supper by the first Christians is provided in the words which are spoken over the bread and wine. The first three gospels place the words spoken at the Last Supper in the framework of a Passover meal which Jesus held with his disciples as a part of his farewell to them (Mark 14:12–16//Matt. 26:17–29//Luke 22:7–23). According to these evangelists, on the eve of Passover Jesus held a farewell meal for his disciples and spoke these words: "This is my body," "This is my blood of the covenant, which is poured out for many." As portrayed in the Gospel of John, however, Jesus' farewell to his disciples does not occur in the context of a Passover meal. According to the Fourth Gospel, Jesus died one day earlier, not on Passover, but on the day before. As the true Passover lamb, he suffered death in the very hour in which the Passover lambs were being killed in the temple (John 18:28; 19:36). The question as to which of these two portrayals gives the correct date can no longer be answered with certainty.

The apostle Paul also gives an account of the Last Supper (1 Cor. 11:23–26), but does not mention the Passover in this connection at all. On the other hand, when he speaks of the Passover, he says nothing about the Lord's Supper, but only that "Christ our Passover lamb, has been sacrificed" (1 Cor. 5:7*). From this we may still infer that Jesus must have been put to death at the time of the

Passover festival in Jerusalem. But whether he died on the festival day itself, or the day before, remains uncertain. The reports of the evangelists emphasize two distinct but related ideas. It is important for the first three evangelists to emphasize that Jesus' last meal took place in the setting of a Passover meal, for in place of the old covenant Jesus had instituted the order of the new covenant, which the disciples celebrated in the Supper. On the other hand, the evangelist John wants to point out that Jesus died on the cross as the true lamb of God and thereby introduced the new age. In sum, the day on which Jesus held the farewell meal with his disciples can no longer be precisely determined. His disciples, however, did continue to celebrate the meal as a continuation of the table fellowship of Jesus, without preserving it as a Passover celebration. The liturgical form of this celebration is determined exclusively by reflection on the death of the Lord and the proclamation of his kingly rule. Therefore, the meaning of the Lord's Supper is not to be derived from its setting within a Passover meal or some other festival assembly, but only from consideration of the words themselves, the words of institution of the Lord's Supper.

The *words of institution* have been handed on in a double tradition, one found in the Gospels of Mark and Matthew, and the other found in Paul's writings and in the Gospel of Luke. A comparison of these two forms, which can be traced back to two different liturgical traditions of the early Christians, allows the meaning of the words to emerge clearly. The words, spoken over the broken bread as it is distributed, read:

"Take, this is my body."
(Mark 14:22//Matt. 26:26*)

"This is my body, which is given for you."
(1 Cor. 11:24//Luke 22:19*)

These words are spoken over the broken bread in order to indicate what is being distributed. All who receive this bread receive a share in the body of Christ given over to death, and therefore in the saving power of his death and resurrection. This meaning of the celebration of the Lord's Supper is also expressed in the words which are spoken over the cup:

"This is my blood of the covenant,
which is poured out for many."
(Mark 14:24//Matt. 26:28*)

"This cup is the new covenant in my blood."
(1 Cor. 11:25//Luke 22:20*)

The reference to the "blood which is poured out" points to the life of Jesus Christ which was given for the benefit of "many"—a Hebrew idiom meaning "all." Christ acted on behalf of all people by paying the debt which they were not able to pay (Mark 10:45). This affirmation is more sharply focused by including the idea of the covenant, which indicates the new way of salvation established by Christ's death. The covenant which was once made on Mt. Sinai was also sealed by the pouring out of blood. It served then to confirm the sealing of the covenant, but it was not able to take away sins (Exod. 24:3–8). The substitutionary death of Christ—this is to be emphasized—is therefore incomparably superior to all the sacrifices of the old covenant. His death establishes the eschatological way of salvation in which there is forgiveness of sins.

In the form of the saying about the cup as it appears in Paul and Luke, the motif of the covenant similarly appears. Here, however, it is described as the new covenant which the prophets promised (Jer. 31:31–34). This new covenant has now become a reality through the substitutionary death of Jesus Christ. It embraces all members of the community and makes them responsible for each other. This is why Paul directs such sharp criticism against the Corinthians. In their congregational meals, the wealthy members had already begun without waiting for the poorer members of the community; they had to come later and could bring nothing with them. So the one feasted while the other had to leave hungry. Paul calls such conduct "unworthy" and warns that God will not leave such unloving and unbrotherly conduct without punishment (1 Cor. 11:27–29). Whoever therefore disdains the body of Christ—this refers both to the body of Christ which was given over to death, and to the church, which is the body of Christ—will be subject to God's judgment. For the Lord wants the members of his body to act out of consideration for each other, to be there for one another.

Many religious groups in the ancient world gathered for cultic meals. In the first century A.D., the worship of Mithras, a light god or sun god, was widespread throughout the Hellenistic world. The worship of Mithras originated in Persia, and portrayed the deity struggling with the bull and killing it, thereby overcoming the powers of darkness which it symbolized. In the many sanctuaries of Mithras, like the ones preserved in Italy, and also in southern Germany, one can still see the sacred room with the cultic picture of the god. The worshipers of Mithras gathered for a common meal, in order to receive the powers of the deity and thereby to become gods themselves. In contrast to such ideas the preaching of the first Christians emphasized that divine power could not be mediated by any such cultic rites and practices, but that at the celebration of the Lord's Supper the death of the Lord is proclaimed, the one who died and was raised "for us." Wherever the Lord's church gathered to confess faith in him and with the bread and wine accepted the heartening declaration of his forgiving act, there the resurrected Lord himself invited his own to his table and united them in the fellowship of the body of Christ.

MISSION

These first Christians understood themselves to be the Israel of God that believes in Jesus as the Christ. All who had been baptized into Christ and called upon his name belonged to God's people. From this awareness the recognition that the people of God cannot remain limited to Jews had to dawn on them: the gospel also had to be proclaimed among the nations, to call them to repentance and faith.

Greek-speaking Jewish Christians who were members of the earliest Jerusalem church became the first missionaries; they first brought the Christian message to the neighboring Samaritans and soon thereafter to other groups of people. The Acts of the Apostles names a group of seven men; their Greek names indicate that they came from the Jewish Diaspora and therefore obviously were already accustomed to freely associating with non-Jews (Acts 6:5). But soon the Jewish faction brought charges against Stephen, the leader of this group, that he was speaking against the Temple and the Law, saying that Jesus would change the regulations which Moses had given (Acts 6:13–14). From this accusation we can see that Stephen must have preached the gospel in such a way that a connection to the Temple and the Law was not a necessary condition for receiving salvation. At the beginning, the earliest church had remained faithful to the Temple (Acts 2:46). Obviously, the first Christians even continued to offer sacrifices in the early days (cf. Matt. 5:23–24) and to pay the Temple tax which every Jew was obligated to pay for support of the holy place (cf. Matt. 17:24–27). This relationship to the Temple was now being severed in the preaching of Stephen. In fact, his preaching could be taken by Jews as an attack on the Mosaic law itself. Therefore, Jewish groups attacked Stephen, seized him, stoned him, and drove his followers out of Jerusalem (Acts 6:8—8:3).

The circle of the Twelve, however, which formed the nucleus of this first Jerusalem church and provided its leadership, was not affected by this persecution. They remained unmolested in Jerusalem (Acts 8:1). The followers of Stephen, by contrast, now turned their attention to Samaria and preached the Christian message there. The Samaritans were not recognized by the Jews as orthodox worshipers of the God of Israel. For that reason Jewish people did not do business with them and sought to avoid contact with them entirely. The Christian message now brought an end to the barrier which had separated Jews and Samaritans. The mission to the Samaritans meant, however, that the fundamental decision for the mission to the Gentile nations had already been made. The path of the Christian message through the Roman world soon led further, so that Christians, whose names we no longer know, founded churches abroad: Damascus, Antioch, along the coast of Palestine, in Rome, and in other places which lay on the great Roman highways connecting the various centers of commerce. This development must have occurred rather quickly, for when Paul became a Christian a few years after Jesus' death there were already churches in Syria with which he could establish contact. This early Christian mission was not set in motion by directives from a central controlling center, but originated through the work of individual Christians and congregations who carried the word from person to person. Because Christ was confessed to be the Lord, each one knew that he or she had received a commission from him to declare his Lordship in the whole world (Matt. 28:18–20). In this way the early Christian missionaries followed the roads which Jewish missionaries, prior to them, had traveled.

The Jewish mission, too, operated without direction from a central organization, but rather functioned by personal contact and the sharing of the faith by one individual with another. The synagogues themselves—widespread due to the Jewish Diaspora—functioned as an effective advertising medium for the Jewish religion. Judaism in the Roman Empire enjoyed the status of a recognized religion, guaranteeing government protection, and was able to establish new synagogues, conduct worship services, and celebrate festivals without hindrance, as well as administer its own laws to its own members and have its own cemeteries. The Jewish worship service, consisting of Scripture readings, psalms, prayers, and oftentimes a sermon, made a great impression on the surrounding non-Jewish world. For one thing, faith in the ancient gods had become widely questioned. It had been replaced by skepticism or a superstitious fear of the threatening powers of fate which supposedly determined the course of the stars and the life of every person.

Judaism knew how to give a clear answer to the questions of life, for it proclaimed the rule of one God who had made the universe and who in the Law had given unambiguous instructions for the conduct of human life. The faith of the Jews was further characterized by the story of Israel's historical origins, shrouded as they were in mystery, and by a venerable tradition. Even if the Jewish way of life was perceived to be peculiar now and then and evoked antipathy, still the attractive aspects outweighed by far the opposition which occasionally arose. Moreover, Judaism had opened itself to Greek ways of thinking, appropriated the Greek language, and had translated the Scriptures into Greek. The moral demands of the Law could for the most part be brought into harmony with philosophical teaching and in this way be made understandable to non-Jews.

At times a rather distinguished group of people gathered around the synagogue to hear the teaching of the Law. Many of these people were prevented by the requirement of circumcision from taking the full step into Judaism and obligating themselves to keep the whole Law. The synagogue sought to meet such seekers halfway, by requiring them to keep only the vitally important Ten Commandments—especially the Sabbath command—and the most important of the dietary laws and ethical demands, and to confess faith in the one God. Whoever accepted these obligations was considered a "God-fearer." Officially, such people remained Gentiles, but they had still entered into a close relationship to the synagogue.

In these circles of the "God-fearers," ones who gathered on the edge of synagogue life, Christian preaching evoked a strong response. Now they heard it proclaimed that the one God had made himself known in his son, through whom he had made salvation available to Jews and Gentiles alike, so that they all would be saved in the coming day of judgment. While it appeared to be a scandalous thing to many Jews that the one who had been crucified was proclaimed as the Messiah of Israel, in those circles of "God-fearing" Gentiles the gospel could be accepted as a liberating proclamation. Through faith in Christ and through baptism they were admitted to the community of the people of God without having to be circumcised and keep the whole Old Testament Law.

The Acts of the Apostles illustrates the effect of early Christian missionary preaching in a series of exemplary stories. In one example, a high official in the treasury department of Candace, the queen of the Ethiopians, had come to Jerusalem to worship (Acts 8:26–40). Obviously, he was a "God-fearer" who wanted to participate in the worship of the God of Israel, although he could not convert to Judaism. On the return trip, while seated in his chariot, he was reading from the book of Isaiah, aloud, as was usual at that time. He was overheard by Philip, a Christian who was passing by. In astonishment, Philip asked him if he understood what he was reading. The official answered, "How can I, unless some one guides me?" At his request, Philip climbed into the chariot and sat beside him. The treasury official had just read a part of Isaiah 53, which speaks of the suffering and death of the servant of God

(Isa. 53:7–8). He turned to Philip with the question, "About whom is the prophet speaking? About himself, or someone else?" With this point of contact, Philip began to preach to him the gospel of Jesus. This preaching made such an impression on the Ethiopian that he responded by accepting the Christian faith. And when they came to a body of water, Philip baptized the official; he continued on his journey with great joy.

Another story deals with the first person in Europe won over to the Christian message by Paul (Acts 16:11–15). In Philippi Paul and his companions went outside the city to a Jewish place of prayer and spoke with the women who gathered there. Among them was a "God-fearer" named Lydia, a businesswoman who dealt in purple goods. She was so immediately moved by the apostle's words that she decided to be baptized, along with her whole house, that is, her family. She invited the messengers of Christ into her house and founded one of the first Christian house churches.

Gentiles, women, and "God-fearers," who had not been able to become members of the people of Israel, accepted early Christian missionary preaching and found themselves together in the newly established churches. These first Christian missionaries mainly turned first to the synagogue and the people who gathered there. This encounter often led to disputes, often resulting in a split of the synagogue congregation. Some accepted the new message, while others rejected it. The well-constructed roads of the Roman empire enabled the missionaries to travel quickly from one place to another. Police and the military protected these great highways. They also secured travel by ship against the danger of attacks from pirates.

Many Jews who lived in the Greek-speaking Diaspora made the transition into the Christian church without any noticeable break. For them, the will of the living God whom Israel was called to serve consisted primarily of ethical conduct. But greater changes were called for by the Gentile Christians. They had to make a clean break with their pre-Christian past, avoid any contact with idolatry, and redirect their whole manner of life in accordance with God's command. This change is described in a brief excerpt from early Christian missionary preaching which is echoed in Paul's letter to the church in Thessalonica. He reminds them "how you turned to God from idols, to serve a living and true God" (1 Thess. 1:9). These words take up the exact content of Jewish missionary preaching, which sought to make clear that, in distinction to the pagan gods, the God of Israel alone is the living and true God—the one that humanity is called to serve. When a Gentile turns from the error and foolishness of his previous way of life to faith in the one true God, the step is taken from darkness into light. Paul, along with other early Christian missionaries, took over such material from Jewish missionary instruction, to which he added in brief the central affirmation of the Christian message: Christians are awaiting God's "Son from heaven, whom he raised from the dead, Jesus who delivers us from the wrath to come" (1 Thess. 1:10). The call for repentance was greatly strengthened by this reference to future divine judgment and the announcement of the near advent of Christ. Whoever turned to Christ in faith would be delivered by him in the coming judgment, and would receive salvation. This preaching of the first Christian missionaries evoked a favorable response from many people.

FOR FURTHER READING

Bainton, Roland. *Early Christianity*. New York: Van Nostrand Reinhold, 1960.

Conzelmann, Hans. *History of Early Christianity*. Nashville: Abingdon Press, 1973.

Cross, Frank M. *The Ancient Library of Qumran and Modern Biblical Studies*. Grand Rapids: Baker Book House, 1980.

Hahn, Ferdinand. *The Worship of the Early Church*. Philadelphia: Fortress Press, 1973.

Interpreter's Dictionary of the Bible, 1962 ed. Entry of "Baptism," by W. F. Flemington.

——, 1962 ed. Entry of "Dead Sea Scrolls," by O. Betz.

——, Supplementary Volume. Entry of "Baptism," by M. Barth.

——, Supplementary Volume. Entry of "Dead Sea Scrolls," by G. Vermes.

Lohse, Eduard. *The New Testament Environment*. Nashville: Abingdon Press, 1976.

4

THE LIFE OF SUFFERING

The Distinctiveness of the First Christians

FAITH

Both Christians and Jews already knew from the Old Testament what it meant to have faith. "If you will not believe, surely you shall not be established" (Isa. 7:9). "The one who believes will not flee" (Isa. 28:16*). Faith means having trust in the promise which God has made to his people with his word. The Christian community confesses that God's own word of encouragement is guaranteed in the gospel. To this proclamation of the love of God, faith responds with a "yes" and acknowledges it as true. And so faith understands that this proclamation is a matter of ultimate concern, because it gives an answer to those questions about the purpose and meaning of life which can never be silenced.

How this answer transforms one's whole life is shown by the example of the apostle Paul. As a Jew, he was proud of his Hebrew origins and had worked hard at fulfilling all the demands of the Law—and with considerable success. It was for this reason that he became an opponent of the Christians and persecuted them, since they had turned aside from the strict Jewish way of life. But the man who had been a zealot for the Law (Gal. 1:13–14; Phil. 3:5–6) was suddenly won over to faith in the crucified Christ. Paul speaks only a few words concerning this decisive moment of his life: "But when he who had set me apart before I was born, and had called me through his grace, was pleased to reveal his Son to me . . . I did not confer with flesh and blood" (Gal. 1:15–16). The event in which he became a Christian is mentioned by Paul only in a subordinate clause. He speaks with careful restraint, because he rests his case neither on his person nor on his experience. The act of God alone is important, an act which is to be traced back to his gracious election. God's call, Paul emphasizes, came to him through the revelation of his son. This means: "I have seen the Lord Jesus" (1 Cor. 9:1); "He appeared also to me" (1 Cor. 15:8). This appearance fundamentally changed his life. Paul says that he once wanted to lift up his own accomplishments before God. But now everything is different. This total transformation is illustrated by a picture which he borrows from the business world. Profit no longer consists of pride in the Law, but only in the fact that he has accepted Christ (Phil. 3:7–9). In faith he has received the gift of divine grace; it also stands at the end of his road: "Not that I have already attained this or am already perfect; but I press on to make it my own, because Christ Jesus has made me his own" (Phil. 3:12).

Because Christ has been acknowledged as Lord by faith, the content of faith can be expressed in the brief formula "that Jesus died and rose again" (1 Thess. 4:14). With extreme terseness these words summarize the foundation of faith: faith is based on the event of the death and resurrection of Jesus Christ. Faith confesses that in this event God himself has acted, and knows therefore that in his death and resurrection we are addressed by God. So the apostle Paul immediately draws this conclusion from his brief reference to the content and ground of faith: If we believe that Jesus died and rose again, then we ourselves are incorporated in this story, which means, "even so, through Jesus, God will bring with him those who have fallen asleep" (1 Thess. 4:14). By this Paul intends to say that all who have placed their trust in Christ as their Lord, and have died in this confidence, will with Jesus attain life from death. They will be caught up into that triumphal procession with him which will unite all who belong to the Lord (1 Thess. 4:13–18). Faith is confident that Christ and his own have been bound inseparably together into a unity which spans past, present, and future.

Whoever believes in the risen Christ receives salvation according to another affirmation of an early Christian creed which Paul incorporated in his letter to the Romans:

> If you confess with your lips that Jesus is Lord,
> and believe in your heart
> that God raised him from the dead,
> you will be saved (Rom. 10:9).

On the one hand, this affirmation (constructed according to a strict parallelism) has conditional clauses—"if you confess" and "if you believe"—which correspond to each other. Faith in the heart and public confession of it are bound closely together, for the element of commitment and obligation inherent in faith comes to expression when it is publicly confessed. On the other hand, the two clauses which express the content of faith also belong most closely together: "Jesus is Lord" and "God raised him from the dead." This means that whoever confesses faith in the crucified and risen Christ confesses him to be the Lord. And conversely, Christ can be confessed as Lord only by those who believe the proclamation of his resurrection from the dead. This confession of faith is proclaimed by the congregation in the worship service, "Jesus is Lord" (1 Cor. 12:3), or "Jesus Christ is Lord" (Phil. 2:11). The only ones who join in this public confession of faith are those who do so in the power of the Spirit, through which they are enabled to acknowledge the crucified Christ as the Lord (1 Cor. 12:1–3). Faith does not therefore originate on the basis of careful weighing of arguments, but from preaching which proclaims Christ and thereby evokes faith (Rom. 10:17).

In order to explain what faith in Christ means, the apostle turns to the Scripture. He appeals to a text from Psalm 143 that says "For no man living is righteous before thee" (that is, before God). Paul makes this statement more pointed by adding the words, "through works of the Law" (Rom. 3:20*). It is beyond the ability of any human being, however religious he or she may be, to establish a right relation to God by his or her own actions. The sense that one is living life as it was meant to be can be had only as a gift of God. Therefore Paul's thesis must read: Therefore "we hold that a man is justified by faith apart from works of law" (Rom. 3:28).

Paul supports his thesis by referring to the story of Abraham, regarded by Jews and Christians alike as the great example of what a truly religious person ought to be. "Abraham believed God, and it was reckoned to him as righteousness" (Gen. 15:6, as quoted in Rom. 4:3 and Gal. 3:6). Paul develops his exposition of the meaning of faith in connection with this text of Scripture. At God's command, Abraham left his homeland and followed God's call into a foreign country. Although he did not know where he would end up, he depended on God's Word—that God would fulfill his promise and give him the land. Sarah and he were already old, but Abraham trusted that God would give them a son and heir. In all this, he had no illusions about the reality of his situation. On the contrary, Abraham by no means overlooked the hard facts which flew in the face of what he had been promised. He rather looked them squarely in the face: his own old body, and the fact that the time had long since passed when it was possible for Sarah to become a mother (Rom. 4:19). Nevertheless, he did not become weak in faith, but continued in the hope that he would become the father of many nations (Rom. 4:18). He thus trusted in the God "who gives life to the dead and calls into existence the things that do not exist" (Rom. 4:17). From this confidence he gained the power to hope against all external appearance, to hope where there appeared to be no basis for hope. Thus Abraham held fast to the promise of God and gave God's power room to work. Because he believed that God's promise was more real than anything else that appeared before his eyes, he came into the only right relationship with God, which is called righteousness. That means—as Paul emphasizes by his appeal to Scripture—that Abraham was set right with God by faith alone.

Paul does not consider Abraham's faith as an isolated event of the past, lying back there in remote history. Rather, Abraham appears as the model of that kind of faith which is still alive in the Christian community, that faith which puts its trust in the gospel of the crucified and risen Christ. The promise given to Abraham is considered to be virtually equivalent to the gospel, for the faith of Abraham, like that of the Christians, depends on nothing else except the word of God spoken to him. Not from seeing, still less from some sort of compelling proof, but exclusively from the power of the Word that encounters him—this is what produces his faith. Therefore Paul explicitly declares that the statement about Abraham's faith being reckoned to him as righteousness was not written for his sake alone, "but for ours also. It will be reckoned to us who believe in him that raised from the dead Jesus our Lord, who was put to death for our trespasses and raised for our justification" (Rom. 4:24–25).

LIFE STYLE

An action-oriented life style emerges from the power of faith. That kind of compulsive busyness, however, which is not fed by this spring, is ultimately useless. This insight is portrayed in a story handed down to us in the Gospel of Luke. Jesus, so the story goes, was visiting with the sisters Mary and Martha in their home. Mary sat at the feet of Jesus to listen to him. Martha, however, had her hands full trying to prepare dinner for Jesus. With some irritation she turned to Jesus and asked if he had not noticed that her sister had left her to work in the kitchen alone. And it was not too late to ask her to help! But Jesus answered that Martha was anxious and fretful about many things: "one thing is needful. Mary has made the better choice. What she has chosen will not be taken away from her" (Luke 10:38–42*). The one thing that is unconditionally necessary is Jesus' word and the faith which responds to it. Faith, however, must be active in love (Gal. 5:6), for whoever believes in Christ as the crucified and risen Lord has been caught up in a movement which determines his or her whole life. As a good tree necessarily bears good fruit, so faith must be active, bring forth fruit, and help other people. Faith must find an outlet in action, because all who confess faith in Christ are called into his service.

This conviction, which seemed obvious to Paul and the earliest Christians, was called into question by some groups in the second Christian generation. There were people who advocated the view that it was sufficient just to have faith, that one's actions made no difference at all. The letter of James, written near the end of the first century A.D., describes the point of view held by these people (James 2:14–26). They apparently said something like: "One person has faith, another has works," in a way which totally separated faith and action. Strangely enough, this view was supported by appealing to statements of Paul, statements which of course had been misunderstood and abbreviated to slogans and catch-phrases. Some asserted that faith alone was all that was necessary in order to be accepted by God. Such acceptance has absolutely nothing to do with works. If one has faith, life can be lived any way one pleases, for "we are justified before God by faith alone."

In such statements there is, in fact, an echo of Pauline sayings.

But these statements of the would-be followers of Paul say nothing about the content of faith. Paul, however, dealt with faith's content with absolute clarity: faith is directed toward Christ and receives from him life and salvation. Only through faith in Christ can one enter into the right relation to God. This fundamental principle of Paul's theology had not been grasped by those people described in the letter of James. They overlooked the consequences of faith which must be worked out in the Christian's life, and simplistically affirmed that faith has nothing to do with life style at all. They thus missed the orientation which faith gives to the whole Christian life: to be at work in deeds of love.

The author of the letter of James rightly rejected as impossible any attempt to separate faith and works. But the reasoning behind his own rejection was of a sort which Paul would not have been able to accept. James, too, refers to the example of Abraham. He believed God, and his faith was reckoned to him as righteousness (Gen. 15:6=James 2:23). James, however, infers from this text of Scripture that faith and works operated together in Abraham's life and that he therefore was justified before God both by faith *and* by works. Faith without works is, of course, dead. To be sure, both Paul and James emphasize that faith must be active. But Paul would never agree that faith and works are two separate activities which can team up to produce righteousness, for God's righteousness can only be received as his gift, not as a reward obtained through human striving. That life style which tries to be obedient to God's command is therefore not a condition for God's gift of salvation. Rather, it is the necessary result of that kind of faith which knows itself to be ruled by the law of Christ, the content of which the apostle can state in brief: "Bear one another's burdens" (Gal. 6:2). This "law of Christ" is not laid down as a compulsory rule to which one must submit with a sigh and a groan. On the contrary, Christians are called by their Lord to a life of freedom. This freedom, however, gives them the opportunity and readiness to serve one another in love: "For the whole law is fulfilled in one word, 'You shall love your neighbor as yourself' " (Gal. 5:14).

The love commandment, which is a summary of all the other commands, is referred to repeatedly by the apostle Paul: "He who loves his neighbor has fulfilled the Law'' (Rom. 13:8). God has given commandments to his people. Paul reminds his readers specifically of a few of them: "You shall not commit adultery, You shall not kill, You shall not steal, You shall not covet" (Rom. 13:9). They are accepted as binding regulations, since they contain God's will and command. But only love, which wills no evil to the neighbor, does what the Law intends. For only love, which is willing to surrender its own interests, fulfills what God, in his holy, righteous, and good Law, both demands and gives. Without love, even the greatest deeds, and all the willingness to give and do, mean nothing (1 Cor. 13:1–3). Where love determines life style, there the relations between people are rightly ordered, and the question of the meaning and purpose of life is persuasively answered.

This answer also comes in a discussion which Jesus once had with a rich young man. He had approached Jesus with the question as to what he should do in order to inherit eternal life (Mark 10:17–22). Jesus gave him the plain answer: "You know the commandments well enough: Do not kill, Do not commit adultery, Do not steal, Do not bear false witness, Do not defraud, Honor your father and mother" (10:19*). By asking this question, the young man obviously intended to say that he was ready to accept some extraordinary task. To his amazement, Jesus instead pointed him to the commandments which he had already known for a long time. By so doing Jesus wanted to say that the will of God is not fulfilled in exceptional accomplishments—not even in exceptionally religious accomplishments—but in the willingness to take God's commands seriously as the norm for everyday life. When the young man was not satisfied with this answer, Jesus identified an option that would put his willingness to do some special deed to the test: "Go, sell what you have, and give to the poor, . . . and come, follow me" (10:21). But—and this is the conclusion of the story— at this word the young man turned away sorrowfully, for he had an abundance of possessions. He was not able to become a follower of Jesus, because he lacked the power to love.

The question of how human life can be responsibly ordered had been continuously pondered not only in Israel but also among the peoples of the ancient Near East and among the Greeks. The first Christians paid careful attention both to the sayings and instructions offered to them by the Jewish tradition and those which had been developed by the Greek philosophers. The apostle Paul once said that Christians should consider this broad stream of Jewish and Greek ethical instruction, and make discriminating judgments: "Whatever is true, whatever is honorable, whatever is just, whatever is pure, whatever is lovely, whatever is gracious, if there is any excellence, if there is anything worthy of praise, think about these things" (Phil. 4:8). But where do Christians find the criteria by which they can determine which rules of conduct should now shape their life style?

The decisive criterion by which the Christian life should be ordered is identified by the apostle Paul at the beginning of that major section in the letter to the Romans which deals with ethical questions. He urges Christians to present their bodies—and that means themselves, in all that they do and are—as living sacrifices, holy and acceptable to God, which is their true act of worship (Rom. 12:1). Cultic ideas—holy, sacrifice, worship—are used here, but in a sense which has left any cultic meaning far behind. Here Paul breaks through the distinction between "holy" and "secular," which was observed everywhere in the ancient world. No longer is there a special holy territory marked off from the ordinary arena of human life. Nor is a sacrificial animal or some other life-form selected to be brought and presented on the altar. Paul speaks rather of the fullness and breadth of human life as the place where Christian action is to be exercised. There is no sacred place which as such is fenced off and treated with the special respect of a consecrated place where sacrifice alone is to be offered. On the contrary, the whole world is the place where the Christians offer their worship in the everyday business of living. In every place where they stand, and at every hour in which they live, they belong to their Lord whom they follow. Thus, Paul continues, they should not submit themselves to the formative power of this world, but should let themselves be shaped by the renewing of their minds, that is, the insightful power of critical judgment. For such renewal—this is the important point to Paul—happens to those who belong to Christ (Rom. 12:2). This personal renewal of which the apostle speaks is a matter of reason, the capacity to think critically and form judgments. While in one place Paul says of the pagans that they became futile in their thinking, and that God turned them over to their irrational minds (Rom. 1:21, 28), here Paul speaks of the renewing activity of God in people's minds, and of action that allows people to make clear, levelheaded judgments in the light of how things really are.

There can be no talk about faith pushing reason aside or even about making reason no longer effective. On the contrary, in faith reason is renewed, recognized as God's gift, and only then is assigned its proper place. It is precisely through the sober view of the world that is opened up to one by Christian faith that the capacity for critical weighing and testing is generated. It is this capacity which allows us to become aware both of reason's possibilities and its limits. With its help, Christians inspect whatever passes in the culture for the rules of right conduct, and place this varied tradition under the scrutiny of the one question: what then is that will of God which is good, acceptable, and perfect (Rom. 12:2)? Although the direction in which God's will points is spelled out with sparkling clarity, in an individual case it can be extremely difficult to decide concretely what is to be done in this particular time and place. Therefore Christians are instructed by the apostle to examine critically the rules of traditional ethics with their renewed powers of judgment under the guidance of the Holy Spirit, in order to decide what really matters (Phil. 1:9–10). Such decisions call for the counsel of one's brothers and sisters in the church. This is why the apostle Paul almost always addressed his letters to the whole church, since Christians are all called together into the same responsibility to follow their Lord in whom they believe, and to live as the commandment of love charges them to do.

MARRIAGE

God created humanity—man and woman (Gen. 1:27). Jesus and the first Christians repeatedly referred to this declaration of the biblical story of creation. In plain language this statement reminds us that there is no such thing as "humanity" in the abstract, but always only man or woman. This order in which our life is set corresponds to the will of the creator. In a vivid picture, Genesis 2 describes how God created man and woman. First he formed Adam from the earth, and then breathed life into him. Then he brought a deep sleep on Adam, took one of his ribs, closed up the incision, and formed woman from the rib. This story intends to portray how man and woman belong together. Only in mutual responsibility to and for each other are they human beings with each other, according to God's will made known in the created order. Because woman is taken from man, she is attracted to him. And the man is to leave father and mother and cleave to his wife. All other human relationships into which one may enter are subordinate to this one. For the sake of the woman, the man gives up his place in the family from which he comes, and joins himself to the woman. And the woman turns to the man and becomes one with him (Gen. 2:24; cf. Matt. 19:5 and 1 Cor. 6:16).

The Old Testament and early Christianity considered the body and human sexuality to be gifts from God, and therefore held them in great respect. Ascetic ideas, of the sort advocated in different ways in Jesus' environment, were foreign to them. The disciples and followers of the Greek philosopher Pythagoras withdrew from the world, and sought to avoid any sort of defilement; on this basis they renounced marriage. And the Jewish community at Qumran, on the shore of the Dead Sea, wanted to maintain a constant state of priestly purity, and therefore chose to live a celibate life. In this way they departed from the understanding of the creation story which was advocated everywhere else in Judaism. It was elsewhere universally regarded as God's command that man and woman should live together in marriage. There were only rare exceptions—such as Jesus and Paul—in which a person did not marry because he was entirely absorbed in some great mission. But Jesus and Paul, too, considered marriage to be a gift of God's creation. Jesus said with regard to marriage, "What therefore God has joined together, let not man put asunder" (Mark 10:9). That means, where man and woman are joined together in marriage, they have entered into the good order established by God, and should not leave it. And Paul quotes the Old Testament saying that man and woman become one flesh, or one body, and adds to it the challenge: "So glorify God in your body" (1 Cor. 6:20).

The apostle Paul was compelled to enter into debate with views which had forced their way into the Corinthian church from the surrounding Greek world. Many members of the church held the view that the body was of less value than the soul or spirit, since it was only the outer hull of the real person. Therefore it did not matter how one let the body behave. One could disdain it, and turn ascetically from the world (1 Cor. 7). Or one could treat the body to luxurious pleasures and indulge it to excess (1 Cor. 6:12–20). Sexual relations with a prostitute only involved the body, not the person himself. Thus one could let the body do as it pleased.

Paul emphatically opposed this view. By no means can the person be split into body and soul, separating the external hull from the real self. Rather, the person is ever and always a unity of body and soul, spirit and physical organs, and this unity in its entirety is God's creation. Therefore "the body is not meant for immorality, but for the Lord, and the Lord for the body" (1 Cor. 6:13). This is a basic principle of the apostle as he explains more closely what it means to belong to the Lord. What a human being is can therefore be really understood only after one's view has been directed to the final goal to which God wants to bring the person: "God raised the Lord and will also raise us up by his power" (1 Cor. 6:14). Resurrection of the dead means that not only the soul but also the whole person as God's creation is called into a new mode of existence. Christ has already been raised up and we shall be raised up with him. Therefore a person's body is to be subjected in obedience to God's will, for it belongs to the Lord. That means it is impossible to live promiscuously, linking up today with this person and tomorrow with someone else. And so Paul raises the question, "Do you not know that your bodies are members of Christ? Shall I therefore take the members of Christ and make them members of a prostitute? Never!" (1 Cor. 6:15). On this subject Paul reminds the Christians, "Do you not know that your body is a temple of the Holy Spirit within you, which you have from God? You are not your own" (1 Cor. 6:19).

Man and woman belong together and are responsible for each other; for "in the Lord woman is not independent of man nor man of woman; for as woman was made from man, so man is now born of woman. And all things are from God" (1 Cor. 11:11–12). Husband and wife should affirm their physical relationship as a gift from God and neither should withhold it from the other. "The wife does not rule over her own body, but the husband does; likewise the husband does not rule over his own body, but the wife does" (1 Cor. 7:4). It can be the case—so Paul suggests—that a husband and wife might agree to suspend having sexual relations for a specified time, in order to devote themselves completely to prayer. But then they should come back together, so that they will not fall into temptation through lack of self-control (1 Cor. 7:5). Paul advises against a full-blown asceticism, because that is precisely the way in which a special danger can develop. Celibacy can be a special gift of God which is given to certain individuals (1 Cor. 7:7), but it cannot be required as a binding rule.

The ancient Near East was acquainted with monogamy and also allowed some forms of polygamy to be legally practiced. Although the Old Testament and Judaism also recognized polygamy as a legal form of marriage, it was rarely practiced in the time of Jesus. In any case, it was only possible for a few rich people to provide for such a large family. Jesus and the first Christians said not a word about whether a man may marry more than one wife. They rather always presuppose that marriage means monogamy, because it conforms to the created order of God.

Adultery was severely punished in the time of Jesus. A woman convicted of adultery could even be punished with death by stoning. The New Testament contains a story of how scribes and Pharisees once brought to Jesus a woman who had been apprehended in the very act of adultery. They pointed out that in the Law Moses had commanded that such women be stoned (cf. Lev. 20:10). But—the story continues—Jesus was not intimidated by their words. He said to them, "Let him who is without sin among you be the first to throw a stone at her" (John 8:7). Much taken aback, they retreated, and slipped away one by one. When they had all disappeared and Jesus found himself alone with the woman whom they had wanted to condemn, he said to her, "Go, and sin no more" (John 8:11*). Thus Jesus exposed all phony self-righteousness by which people exalt themselves over others and want to be their judges. But also, for that person who through her own guilt had fallen into distress, he made possible a new beginning. "Sin no more" means that mistakes of the past are marked out; now all that counts is the new beginning which Christ gives to those who trust in him.

In the Judaism of those days it was no great difficulty to dissolve a marriage—only from the husband's side of course. The Old Testament prescribes: if someone takes a wife and she does not find favor in his eyes, because he finds some indecency in her, then he should write her a bill of divorce, place it in her hand, and send her out of his house (Deut. 24:1). Some scribes regarded it to be sufficient grounds for divorce if a woman was not a good cook—if she burned the food or salted it too much. Jesus opposed such views of divorce, and in fact prohibited it entirely (Mark 10:9) for marriage binds husband and wife together until death parts them.

Among the first Christians these words of Jesus were regarded as valid teaching, but they were not considered to be a rigid law. In his letter to the Corinthians Paul deals with questions about marriage and divorce which had arisen in the congregation, and refers first to this saying of Jesus (1 Cor. 7:10). Then he discusses cases in which a marriage could possibly be in danger. It is difficult when one partner has become a Christian and the other has not. If the unbelieving partner is willing to continue in the marriage, then it should not be dissolved. Through the Christian partner, holiness is communicated to the unbelieving partner, who is thereby brought within the arena where the gospel is effective (1 Cor. 7:12–14). But it is a different matter if the unbelieving partner does not want to continue the marriage. Then the Christian should not attempt to restrain the other partner, but let him or her go (1 Cor. 7:15). Thus Paul does not close his eyes to the fact that under certain conditions the continuation of a marriage is no longer possible. Then the man or woman should not remain bound as with chains, for "God has called us to peace" (1 Cor. 7:15). The evangelist Matthew and the congregations in which he lived named adultery and other forms of sexual immorality as grounds on which a marriage could be dissolved (Matt. 5:32; 19:9). This, of course, does not remove the command that man should not put asunder what God has joined together. But there may be situations in which the order established by God breaks apart by the culpable failure of human beings.

The partnership of man and woman takes on an extraordinarily profound meaning in the letter to the Ephesians. Just as Christ gave himself for the church, in order that he might present it holy and without blemish, so men ought to love their wives as their own bodies (Eph. 5:25–28). Through the love of Christ, in which one person encounters another, human love is shared and confirmed. Because the love of Christ bears all things, believes all things, hopes all things, and endures all things (1 Cor. 13:7), man and woman should not live together "in the passion of lust like heathen who do not know God," but "in holiness and honor" (1 Thess. 4:4–5).

POLITICS

Jesus and the earliest Christians were not able to exercise any influence on the political events of their time. A Roman governor ruled Judea. Throughout the empire, the government authorities determined what could be done and what could not be done. Those who possessed Roman citizenship enjoyed the special protection of the official agencies. As a special honor, citizenship was sometimes conferred on various municipalities, so that, for example, the apostle Paul was a citizen from birth (Acts 16:37; 22:27). A Roman citizen could not be punished with scourging, or, in case of a death sentence, with crucifixion. The subjected populations, however, possessed no political rights, but had to comply with the directions of the Roman officials. The Jews of Palestine suffered under Roman occupation. Devout people hoped for the day when the pagan government would disappear. Some groups, however, planned violent action by which the Romans would be driven out. The attacks which they attempted against the Roman soldiers always ended in failure and bloodshed, but nevertheless the level of restlessness and dissatisfaction among the Jewish population continued to mount. The Gospels report that one day some Pharisees came to Jesus and presented him with a problem in order to embarrass him. They asked him whether it was right to pay taxes to the emperor or not (Mark 12:13–17). How should Jesus respond? If he were to say that it was not right, he would have become immediately suspect as an agitator and would have been arrested. But if he had said that taxes should in fact be paid to the emperor, he would henceforth be seen in a bad light by every Jew, for he would be declaring himself to be in support of the pagan occupation force and separating himself from his own people. The story reports that Jesus penetrated the trickiness of their question and asked for a coin. Then he asked, "Whose likeness and inscription is this?" Jewish coins were decorated with designs and symbols, but not with the image of a ruler, for the law was followed which prohibited the making of images (Exod. 20:4). Greek and Roman coins, however, always depicted the head of the ruler who exercised political authority. The inscription gave his name and official title. The Roman coins current in Palestine at that time bore the image of the emperor. So the response to Jesus' question had to be "Caesar's." To this Jesus replied, "Render to Caesar the things that are Caesar's, and to God the things that are God's" (Mark 12:17). Jesus did not fall into the trap which had been set for him, but plainly described the political reality of his time and thereby revealed the distinction between God's kingdom and earthly kingship. The emperor rules the country; that cannot be disputed. But whoever really gives to God what belongs to him— one's self, one's whole life, thinking, and doing—will also be able to give the emperor what is due him.

This calm view of things also determined the attitude of the first Christians to the secular authorities. In his letter to the church in Rome, the apostle Paul encouraged Christians to be subject to those who exercised the powers of government (Rom. 13:1), for the current civil power comes from God. Those who govern administer a power which is ultimately of divine origin. One must comply with their directives; for the civil authority does not bear the sword in vain. It is God's servant. In their own conscience, citizens must acknowledge the order it establishes, and, of course, they pay customs and taxes. In the same way, they show

respect to whom respect is due and honor to whom honor is due
(Rom. 13:1–7).

This text expressed a positive attitude toward the secular political order. It is to be acknowledged and even honored. It is established by God and therefore has every right to demand that all
citizens follow its orders and laws. These comments from the letter
to the Romans are, of course, stated in general terms and reveal no
specifically Christian line of argument. Paul speaks neither of
Christ, nor of grace, love, or compassion, but simply declares what
applies to people generally. In a similar way, instruction was given
in the Jewish synagogue as to how one should conduct oneself in
relation to the secular authorities. In such instruction, language
which was understandable by and acceptable to as many people as
possible was used. Thus the notion of "conscience" was used, a
notion foreign to the Old Testament. In picking up "conscience," a
term which had been coined in the philosophical discussion of the
ancient world was adopted. Conscience was understood as that
critical inner voice in every person which says what should be done
and what should be avoided. It obligates each person to fulfill the
duties involved in being a responsible member of society; it is a
matter of fulfilling obligations incumbent on people generally. If
this expectation is met, one may anticipate that the civil authorities
will express approval and will honor worthy citizens. Whoever
does good will be praised; the evil will receive just punishment.

In Rom. 13:1–7 we have a good example of how the first Christians were educated in the broad stream of moral instruction already developed in the ancient world and how they adopted time-
tested rules of conduct from it. Such instructions first received a
Christian character by the context in which they were now placed:
Christians are called to give themselves as a living, holy sacrifice
which is pleasing to God (Rom. 12:1–2). By carrying out their true
worship of God in the arena of the everyday world, Christians, in
fulfilling their daily tasks, signify that they worship the God and
Father of Jesus Christ in all of their lifelong activities.

The Roman Empire was well organized and administered. Of
course it still repeatedly happened that the governors and officials
laid heavy burdens on the people of their territories in order to

squeeze out as much money as possible and thus dealt unjustly with people. Nevertheless, the Roman power succeeded in bringing law and order to all parts of the empire, putting down uprisings and maintaining the peace. What happened in the capital city was of little concern to the people in the provinces, and hardly affected their everyday lives. Christians too acknowledged this order. The general rule was "Fear God, honor the emperor" (1 Pet. 2:17). Christians were to be submissive to rulers and authorities, to fulfill their obligations, and to be ready to do any honest work (Titus 3:1).

Along with this understanding of right conduct in public life, the boundary was also marked off: "We must obey God rather than men" (Acts 5:29). When orders are given which conflict with God's command, then God must be obeyed and every other claim rejected. The Christians encountered just such a situation during the reign of the emperor Domitian (A.D. 81–96). He demanded that divine honors should be paid to him throughout the empire. For centuries people in the ancient Near East had been accustomed to viewing the ruler as a manifestation of the deity. Such ideas had also found their way to Rome and had already influenced the emperor Nero (A.D. 54–68), although he had not been able to put them into effect; now such ideas were taken up again by Domitian. The worship of the emperor was intended to unify—by a common bond—a multitude of different peoples and cultures in the empire. Every citizen was expected to offer a small bit of incense on the altar and thereby certify that the divine majesty of the emperor was acknowledged. At the great festivals in Rome which Domitian sponsored, he enjoyed having the crowds greet him and his wife with the acclamation, "Hail to our Lord and our Lady!" And when he sent out official decrees, he spoke with divine authority, choosing for the introductory words, "Our Lord and God commands the following." Whoever hesitated to acknowledge these divine honors met with his wrath. This is the background situation of the Revelation to John, written near the end of the first century A.D., in Asia Minor. Christians too were commanded to pay homage to the emperor and to honor him as a manifestation of the divine. They knew, of course, that they should respect the law and order of society as represented by the emperor, but they could not yield to the command to acknowledge the ruler as a god (Revelation 12—13). Christ alone is "King of kings and Lord of lords" (Rev. 19:16). They could pay this honor to no one else. So they too were persecuted because of their refusal. Because they chose to obey God rather than men, they were prepared to walk the path of martyrdom.

SUFFERING

"If any man would come after me," so said Jesus, "let him deny himself and take up his cross and follow me" (Mark 8:34). No other destiny awaited Jesus' disciples than that of their Lord. Whoever says "I do not know this man" (Mark 14:71) thereby rejects him and denies that he or she belongs to him. But whoever is not ashamed to stand with the one who is despised by others thereby confesses that he or she belongs to him (Rom. 1:16). So when it is said that those who follow Jesus must be willing to deny themselves, that means that they have renounced all the security given by property and possessions, and have directed their gaze entirely to their Lord. The one who follows Jesus must be prepared to meet one's end on the cross, just like Jesus.

The future which Jesus' disciples face is described in unadorned plainness. They may not anticipate successes and victorious accomplishments, but "they will deliver you up to councils; and you will be beaten in synagogues; and you will stand before governors and kings for my sake . . ." (Mark 13:9). And to Christians who must take such suffering upon themselves, it is said, "And when they bring you to trial and deliver you up, do not be anxious beforehand what you are to say; but say whatever is given you in that hour, for it is not you who speak, but the Holy Spirit" (Mark 13:11). Even in the most extreme circumstances which Jesus' disciples might encounter, they need not feel abandoned. The Spirit of God will be with them, and will give them the words with which they can testify to their faith.

The first persecutions directed against the Christians came from the Jews. Disputes repeatedly broke out in the synagogues when Christians spoke there and expressed their faith in Jesus. Any Jewish male could exercise his right to make a speech in the congregational worship service. But when Jewish Christians in the synagogue proclaimed "that it was necessary for the Christ to suffer and to rise from the dead" (Acts 17:3), some people responded by accepting what they had said, but most resisted and rejected the message. Therefore Paul had to leave the synagogue in Thessalonica (Acts 17:4–9), and a short time later was driven out of the synagogue in Corinth (Acts 18:1–8). He was dragged before the judgment seat of the Roman governor in the province of Achaia and he was charged: "This man is persuading men to worship God contrary to the law" (Acts 18:13). Roman officials were usually hesitant to get involved in the internal concerns of the Jewish communities (so Acts 18:14–17). However, when quarrels arose which threatened to disturb the peace, the decision usually went against the weaker faction, and the Christians were forced to leave the synagogue. The final separation between synagogue and church did not take place, however, until near the end of the first century. At that time a curse on Jewish Christians and heretics was introduced into the daily Jewish prayer and also was recited in every worship service: "Let there be no hope for the apostates . . . let the Nazarenes and the heretics be destroyed in a moment, blotted out from the Book of Life and not listed among the righteous." This made it absolutely impossible for a Jewish Christian to continue participating in synagogue worship, for he could not pronounce such a curse on himself. The Gospel of John, written near the turn of the century, presupposes that this separation had already taken place. Whoever confessed Jesus as the Christ was expelled from the synagogue (John 9:22; 12:42; 16:2). But this meant that Christians also lost the protection of the Roman government which they had enjoyed as members of Judaism, a religion with official status in the empire.

The civil authorities, of course, did not immediately notice that the Christians were no longer a sect within Judaism, but adherents of a new religion. At first the kind of conflicts which took place between Christians and Jews seem to have been regarded by them as inner-Jewish disputes. The Roman author Suetonius reports that the emperor Claudius—probably in the year A.D. 49—drove the Jews out of Rome "because they were causing riots at the instigation of a certain Chrestus." This comment is the oldest reference to the beginnings of a Christian community in the imperial capital. Its content is vague, and it has obviously confused "Christ" (Latin *Christus*) with a common name of that time, "Chrestus," who is taken for a person still alive in A.D. 49. But this comment does inform us that conflicts arose between Jews and Jewish Christians as a result of the introduction of the Christian message in Rome. Thereafter, since Jewish Christians obviously were driven out of Rome along with other Jews, the Roman church consisted for the most part of Gentile Christians.

During the reign of the emperor Nero, the Roman church was struck by the first great persecution of Christians. This fact is reported by the second-century Roman historian, Tacitus, who disdained Christians as adherents of a superstitious religion, but let his empathy for their fate be clearly seen. Many houses in Rome had been destroyed by a great fire. The rumor circulated in the city that Nero himself had the fire started. In order to draw attention away from himself, the emperor sought to direct the wrath of the people to a group who, as a disliked minority, could not protect themselves. Tacitus further states in his *Histories,*

> Therefore, in order to make an end of this rumor, he pushed the guilt off on others, and punished them with the most exquisite tortures. There were these people who were already hated by the people because of their foul deeds, who were called "Christians." This name comes from "Christ," who had been executed by the governor Pontius Pilate in the reign of Tiberius. This hateful superstition was suppressed for the moment, but later broke out again, and spread not only through Judea where it originated, but also to Rome, where every detestable and abominable thing flows and is practiced. First those were arrested who openly professed to be Christians, then, with information obtained from them, an immense mass of people. They were convicted less of arson than of hatred for the whole human race. They were executed in mocking, derisive ways. Some were covered with animal skins, and torn to pieces by wild dogs. Others were crucified, or, having been condemned to death by fire, were burned after dark for illumination. Nero made his own gardens available for this spectacle, and arranged a circus at the same time, at which, dressed as a charioteer, he mingled among the people or stood in his chariot.

The apostle Peter probably was one of the many victims of this persecution. At about the same time Paul was also brought as a prisoner from Jerusalem to Rome, and was executed after his unsuccessful appeal. Accurate accounts of his death no longer exist. About the end of the first century A.D. the first letter of Clement, written in Rome, incidentally mentions that Peter and Paul had died courageously as apostles, having received the victor's crown of patient endurance.

During the reign of the emperor Domitian (A.D. 81–96), once again the Christian community was dangerously threatened, because they resisted the emperor's demand that he be honored as a god. This danger must have been especially acute in Asia Minor. There was the expectation of an "hour of trial which is coming on the whole world, to try those who dwell upon the earth" (Rev. 3:10). In some communities Christians were put to death (Rev. 2:13), and churches prepared for the worst. In all this, the Christians were aware that during the last times they would have to face bitter troubles and persecution (Mark 13:14–23). But when Domitian was murdered in A.D. 96, the danger passed by. That is, the Christians no longer had to fear a general persecution sponsored by the state. Yet in everyday affairs they had to endure much scorn and abuse from those outside the churches.

The first letter of Peter, written near the end of the first century in the name of the revered apostle, has this situation in view. It encourages Christians to accept suffering willingly when it comes, for in this they are following their Lord, who did not respond with abusive words when he was reviled, and did not "threaten" when he had to suffer (1 Pet. 2:23). It is therefore a matter of conducting oneself in such a way as to avoid bringing reproach on the whole community of Christians, and of suffering for the sake of good deeds (1 Pet. 2:20). They are blessed if they suffer for righteousness' sake (1 Pet. 3:14). Therefore Christians should not be afraid when they are insulted or treated with contempt, but should always be prepared to give an answer to anyone who calls them to account for the hope that is in them (1 Pet. 3:15).

HOPE

Through their hope, Christians were distinguished from the surrounding world, where for the most part people lived without hope.

In the first letter to the Thessalonians, the apostle Paul wrote to this church which he had founded that he did not want to leave them uninformed "concerning those who are asleep, that you may not grieve as others do who have no hope" (1 Thess. 4:13). When the young Christian community experienced its first cases of death, the question was raised whether those who had died would still participate in the future salvation—or whether they would be left out. Paul wanted to show the church that Christians know, by the power of faith, that death does not mean the end. "For since we believe that Jesus died and rose again, even so, through Jesus, God will lead those who have fallen asleep to a new life with him" (1 Thess. 4:14*). All who have died in faith in Christ belong to him in a way which can never be destroyed. Rather, they shall be raised and be united with their Lord who will appear visibly at the end of time.

In the church at Corinth, the question was raised even more sharply than at Thessalonica. There, some people in the congregation completely rejected the Christian hope for the future. "There is no resurrection of the dead"—this thesis expressed their opposing view that they wanted the whole church to accept (1 Cor. 15:12). Paul resisted this view by reminding the congregation that they had come to faith by accepting the proclamation of the crucified and risen Christ (1 Cor. 15:3–5). The Christian hope of the resurrection of the dead is thus based on the content of the Christian confession itself; for as Christ has triumphed over death, his own will not remain in death, but will be raised up. Paul therefore argues neither on the basis of general reflections concerning the possibility of life beyond death, nor from the ideas about resurrection which had been developed in the eschatological expectations of contemporary Judaism, but rather presupposes that he speaks to Christians who are ready to hear conclusions based on the Christian message itself. It is not wishful thinking, or a vague set of human hopes, which creates and nourishes the confidence that God will give life to the dead, but faith in Christ alone. Thus Paul's response: "Now if Christ is preached as raised from the dead, how can some of you say that there is no resurrection of the dead?" (1 Cor. 15:12). Once it is accepted that Christ is the risen Lord, it can no longer be disputed that the dead are raised. Otherwise, one would be in the position of denying that Christ himself was raised, and the very basis of the Christian faith itself would be surrendered.

What follows from this approach which Paul has chosen for his debate? The conceptual possibility that there could be no such thing as a resurrection of the dead, and therefore Christ could not have been raised, is dismissed by the apostle with a wave of the hand (1 Cor. 15:20–28). This theoretical possibility is not to be taken seriously, for the fact of the matter is that Christ has been raised from the dead, and not as an isolated peculiarity but as the first fruits of all those who have fallen asleep. With this expression Paul alludes to a practice prescribed in the Old Testament, that the first sheaves of the harvest were to be brought to the Temple (Lev. 23:10). This presentation of the first sheaves was a sign that the entire produce of the land belonged to God. Thus when Christ is described as the "first fruits," this means that as the resurrected one he represents the whole of humanity. When Christ was raised up, this was the beginning of the resurrection of the dead as such. Because the first one has been raised from the dead, the others will be also. The affirmation that the dead will be raised is grounded exclusively on the proclamation of the resurrection of Jesus Christ. Its truth is demonstrated only in the authority inherent in the power of preaching itself. All human working and living move relentlessly toward death. But since Christ did not remain in death, death will not have the last word.

The New Testament nowhere gives descriptions or pictures of just what the future blessedness for which Christians hope will be like; only promises of the coming glory are given in order to awaken faith. Where this word is not believed, signs and wonders would also do no good, as illustrated in a parable. Before the door of a rich man lay a poor man named Lazarus, who in his misery could only eat the scraps from the rich man's table. When the poor man died, he was taken by the angels to Abraham's bosom. The rich man also died, and woke up in Hades—in hellish pain. When he saw Abraham far off, and Lazarus in his bosom, he asked that Abraham might send Lazarus to him, just to dip his finger in water and cool his tongue. But this request was denied, because he had justly been assigned to eternal torment. Then in his distress the rich man uttered one last request: would Abraham send Lazarus to his five brothers, to warn them, so that they would not come to this place of torment? But this request too was rejected: "They have Moses and the prophets; let them hear them" (Luke 16:29). Even the miracle of someone who had died being sent back to this world would not cause them to repent (Luke 16:19–31).

The gospel alone is the basis of hope and the possibility of renewal. Whoever trusts this message receives eternal life. This gift of eternal life is a very important topic in the Gospel of John. It is not understood as something one receives in the great hereafter, but as a reality already experienced in the here and now. The Johannine Christ says: "Truly, truly, I say to you, he who hears my word and believes him who sent me, has eternal life; he does not come into judgment, but has passed from death to life" (John 5:24). This text, introduced by a formula of solemn assurance, speaks of life, death, and judgment. The thought here is not about a future event which will occur at the end of history. It does not describe that judgment of all people on the last day, but it describes what happens when a person heeds Jesus' word and opens himself or herself to it in faith. He or she acknowledges Jesus to be the one whom the Father has sent into the world as its savior. Whoever turns to him in trust and accepts his word as true thereby takes the step by which everything is decided, or rather has already been decided. Such a person can no longer come into judgment and can be condemned by no one.

The other side of this reality is clear: "He who does not believe is condemned already, because he has not believed in the name of the only Son of God" (John 3:18). So the last judgment is also already happening wherever anyone rejects the love of God which is presented to him or her in Christ. But faith knows itself to be so firmly bound to God through Christ, that neither pain nor suffering, neither death nor a sinful life is able to separate us from him (Rom. 8:38–39). Thus the New Testament teaches: whoever believes that has already passed over from death to life and does not come into judgment.

This reality of faith is expressed in a Johannine saying of Christ: "I am the resurrection and the life; he who believes in me, though he die, yet shall he live, and whoever lives and believes in me shall never die" (John 11:25–26). This means that resurrection and life are not independent realities which one may have apart from Christ, but are received only as Christ, who is the resurrection and the life, is trusted and accepted. Thus Jesus does not promise this or that gift to people, but himself. Whoever therefore believes in Christ as the resurrection and the life will live, even though the reality of earthly death must still be faced. And whoever lives and believes in him will never die. Of course, he or she remains subject to physical death and must endure it. But the power of life which Christ gives to his own cannot be destroyed, not even by death. For those who belong to Christ, death has lost its character of having ultimate power. This does not mean, of course, that suffering, trouble, and pain are eliminated, but the terror of death has been taken away, because Christ has been raised up to a life which can never be destroyed by death. Because he shares his own life with those who believe, they have already put death behind them, although they still must die. "Do you believe this?" asks Jesus (John 11:26). He is not asking whether we understand the concepts involved, or if our reason grasps what is said; for only in faith can the basis for such hope be recognized. And so the answer is clear: "Yes, Lord; I believe that you are the Christ, the Son of God, he who is coming into the world" (John 11:27).

FOR FURTHER READING

Bonhoeffer, Dietrich. *The Cost of Discipleship*. New York: Macmillan Co., 1967.

Bornkamm, Günther. *Paul*. New York: Harper & Row, 1971.

Gollwitzer, Helmut. *Song of Love: A Biblical Understanding of Sex*. Philadelphia: Fortress Press, 1979.

Hermission, Hans-Jürgen, and Lohse, Eduard. *Faith*. Nashville: Abingdon Press, 1981.

Kaiser, Otto, and Lohse, Eduard. *Death and Life*. Nashville: Abingdon Press, 1981.

Kysar, Myrna, and Kysar, Robert. *The Asundered: Biblical Teachings on Divorce and Remarriage*. Atlanta: John Knox Press, 1978.

5

THE CHRISTIAN'S BASIC DOCUMENT

The Distinctiveness of the Biblical Writings

LETTERS

The composition of a letter in biblical times is hardly to be compared with the way they are written in our own day. In the ancient world, letters were usually kept very brief. The average extent of a letter was about two hundred and fifty words. The entire contents could thus be copied on a single page. A reed pen, dipped in a thick ink, was used for writing. After the message was written, the sheet of papyrus was rolled up, tied, and sealed. The name and address of the receiver was copied on the outside of the letter. The letter was frequently dictated to a secretary. Then the greeting at the end of the letter would be written in the sender's own hand, so that the receiver could be assured that it had really been written by the sender. The official postal service was not available for private correspondence, so letters had to be entrusted to travelers.

The Acts of the Apostles gives an example of the outline and content of an ancient letter. Paul has been imprisoned in Jerusalem. The Roman officer in charge sends the prisoner under guard to the governor at Caesarea, and gives the soldiers an accompanying letter. The text of this letter comprises only five verses of the New Testament (Acts 23:26–30). It begins with the usual introduction, containing both the name of the sender and the receiver, and a greeting: "Claudius Lysius to his excellency the governor Felix, Greeting." The letter then reports how Paul had been attacked by the Jews who tried to kill him. But the author of the letter had intervened when he learned that Paul was a Roman citizen. The attempt to determine the reason for the attack by bringing Paul before the Jewish council had been unsuccessful. Therefore Paul is being sent to Caesarea in protective custody, and his accusers have been advised to present their case directly to the governor.

The apostle Paul, author of the oldest writings contained in the New Testament, made use of the customary letter form of the ancient world. He moved from place to place, founding churches in which former Jews and Gentiles now found themselves together. As the messenger of the resurrected Lord he had brought to them the gospel, which they had received in faith. His word was intended to strengthen the new Christians, so that they could live their lives responsibly. They needed this word even when the apostle had found it necessary to move on to a different locality. In order to remain in contact with the new churches, to answer new questions which suddenly arose, or to make and communicate necessary decisions, Paul wrote letters. At the beginning of his letters Paul placed his name, to which he added the name of the receivers. His greeting was consistently, "Grace to you and peace" (1 Thess. 1:1). "Grace" refers to the act of God accomplished in Christ. And "peace" is the new reality which he had brought into being by the death and resurrection of Christ. These heartening words which stand at the beginning of every Pauline letter are referred to again at the conclusion: "The grace of our Lord Jesus Christ be with you" (1 Thess. 5:28). Preceding these final words are usually found greetings to individual people or groups in the congregation. Several times an instruction is also found, "Greet all the brethren with a holy kiss" (1 Thess. 5:26). This expression refers to a part of the early Christian liturgy. After the reading of the Scripture, sermon, singing of Psalms, and prayer had prepared for the celebration of the Eucharist, the worshipers declared the forgiveness of all sins to each other, and as a sign thereof exchanged the brotherly kiss. Thus Paul sent his letters to the churches with the intention that they be read aloud to the congregation during the worship service. This was done during the time in the service usually filled with teaching and preaching. After that, the celebration of the Lord's Supper took place, in which the whole congregation was joined together in familial fellowship.

When the letters were not too long, Paul certainly wrote them with his own hand. Still, all the Pauline letters are much more extensive than the normal personal letters of his time. The shortest of the apostle's writings is the letter to Philemon. Although addressed primarily to an individual member of the church, at the same time Paul also addresses the whole congregation. Paul writes from prison, the location of which we cannot be sure. The slave Onesimus has run away from his master and has sought refuge with Paul. But the apostle cannot possibly keep him. Paul too must respect the property rights of Philemon, the owner. So he sends the runaway slave back. But with him he sends a letter to Philemon, to help pave the way for a kindly reception. The letter says nothing about granting Onesimus his freedom, or of the abolition of slavery as such. Nor does the apostle issue any commands, although he—as he says—would be justified in giving binding instructions by virtue of his apostolic authority. He rather makes requests on behalf of Onesimus, who had become very dear to him. When Philemon receives him back, he should receive him as one who is much more than a slave. He should welcome him back as a beloved brother, as if the apostle himself came to him. To be sure, one of them remains the master, and the other the slave. But the determining factor in the person-to-person relationship now is love, which causes its renewing power to be felt in changing the relationships between people, so that each now stands before the other as a brother in the common faith.

The longer letters which Paul sent to the churches were not written by his own hand but dictated. This is indicated by a brief comment at the end of the letter to the Romans. Included in the lengthy list of greetings is found this brief statement: "I Tertius, the writer of this letter, greet you in the Lord" (Rom. 16:22). He obviously used a pause in the dictation to insert a personal greeting. Paul also understands his work as a writer to be in the service of Christ. Long letters such as those sent to the churches in Corinth and Rome could not possibly have been outlined and written in one day. Their composition certainly took a considerable time, and they could only have been written with the help of a patient scribe. The apostle Paul addressed the churches as their preacher and teacher. This is why his letters are much more extensive and richer in content than the typical letters of his day.

The oldest Pauline letter is his first writing to the church in Thessalonica, probably written in the year A.D. 50. The church had been founded by the apostle after he had transferred his missionary work from Asia Minor to Europe and had come from Philippi to Thessalonica, the capital of the Roman province of Macedonia. According to the portrayal in Acts (17:1–15), Paul first preached for three Sabbaths in the synagogue, with only minimal results. Then he was driven out by the Jews, and turned his attention to the Gentiles. But the uproar caused by the Jews made it necessary for him to leave town shortly thereafter. Since Paul wanted to strengthen the young church, he sent his coworker, Timothy, to them. He returned to the apostle with new reports (1 Thess. 3:1, 5) which prompted Paul to write to the church.

The first part of the letter is a long, drawn-out statement of thanksgiving. It corresponds to the ancient letter style, in which the introductory greeting was followed by a thanksgiving to the gods because they had graciously brought the recipient through some danger, or had proven to be helpful through this or that favor. Paul, however, thanks God, the Father of Jesus Christ, whom he addresses in prayer, and to whom he remembers the church. He includes in the thanksgiving a report of how the young congregation is getting along, having endured all the hostilities and temptations to which it had been subjected (1:2—2:16), and a description of his experiences since he had last been with the church (2:17—3:13). This thanksgiving section of the letter concludes with a summary prayer that the Lord will make them increase and become richer and richer in love for each other and for all people.

After the extended thanksgiving Paul switches over to ethical exhortation (4:1–12; 5:12–24) and responds to two questions which the church had put to him (4:13—5:11). This didactic section deals with the form of Christian life to which the early Christian church should conform in its everyday dealings. The questions which Timothy had brought with him on his return from Thessalonica refer to ambiguities which had developed in the light of the eschatological expectations of the community. As a result of the sudden death of some members of the church, anxiety had arisen concerning whether the dead would participate in the future salvation, or whether they would be excluded. Paul responds to this question by taking up a word of the Lord from the oral tradition which declared that when the Lord comes, those who are asleep will be raised, and together with the living will go to meet the returning Lord. Then they will be with him forever (4:13–18). A second question directed to the apostle also concerns the events of the last time. And Paul's answer is that Christians should be awake and alert, ready for the coming of the Lord at any time (5:1–11).

Obviously, Paul succeeded in answering the questions of the church to their satisfaction, for they preserved his letter, certainly read it repeatedly in their worship services, and shared it with other churches. Not all the letters written by the apostle have been preserved. Thus 1 Cor. 5:9, 11 refer to a lost letter to the Corinthians. And Col. 4:16 speaks of a letter to the Laodiceans of which nothing else is known: the church at Colossae should share their letter with the church in Laodicea and obtain a copy of the letter written to the Laodiceans for their own use. From these comments we learn that the churches generally exchanged apostolic letters. Very early, copies would have been made of them, in order to preserve the apostle's word. This is why quite early—apparently the larger churches of Corinth and Ephesus took the lead in this—collections of Pauline letters came into being. At the beginning of the second century, the major Pauline letters were already known everywhere in Asia Minor, and soon thereafter to churches in other areas. They were read repeatedly in order to hear what the witness of the resurrected Lord had to say to the churches.

GOSPEL

When the apostle Paul wrote his letters, there were not yet in existence any of those books later called Gospels. The church's message from and about Jesus was transmitted orally. When Paul introduces words of the Lord—for example in his response to the church in Thessalonica (1 Thess. 4:13–18)—he presents material which he has taken from the oral tradition. The record of what Jesus had taught, done, and suffered did not begin to be written until about forty years after Jesus' death. Even so, the evangelist Mark, who was the first to put the tradition in written form, composed his Gospel before the destruction of Jerusalem by the Romans (A.D. 70), for in distinction from the other Gospels which originated later, the speech predicting doom for the Temple and city (Mark 13) gives no indication that the announcement of the divine judgment has already been fulfilled.

The evangelist Mark introduces his work by the title: "The beginning of the gospel of Jesus Christ" (1:1). He intends therefore to speak of the gospel, and this gospel had its historical beginning at the beginning of the public ministry of Jesus. The first readers of this book had no difficulty in understanding what this means, for the word "gospel," which means nothing more or less than "good news," was already used elsewhere in the Greek-speaking world. An inscription from the year 9 B.C. has been discovered in Priene in Asia Minor. Its content refers to Caesar Augustus, to whom divine honors were paid in Asia Minor. The inscription contains these words: "The birthday of the god was for the world the beginning of the good news" (same Greek word as "gospel"). Further events in his life which were described as good news were the announcements of the ruler's coming of age, his coronation, and his victories. These events, understood as deeds of the god, were to be praised in the whole empire, for in the manifestation of the divine ruler, heavenly glory was visible.

The understanding of the word "gospel" inherent in early Christian preaching was different from this, in that a number of different events were not reported as "gospels," but there was only one gospel: the proclamation of the act of God which happened in the death and resurrection of Jesus Christ (1 Cor. 15:3–5). Beside this one gospel, there can be no other (Gal. 1:6–9). The good news proclaimed in the Christian message is therefore inseparably bound up with the story of Jesus Christ. In him, the reality has appeared which was promised in the prophetic writings of the Old Testament (Rom. 1:2–4). He himself is the messenger of good news, who proclaims that with his appearance the words of the prophets are fulfilled (Luke 4:18–21). Those who heard this preaching were invited to respond to it in faith.

The evangelist Mark, along with early Christians in general, understood the concept "gospel" as the proclamation of the crucified and risen Christ. This is why the narrative about Jesus' path to suffering and death dominates Mark's portrait of the Christ (Mark 11—15), and why it concludes with the Easter message. But the evangelist has broadened the meaning of the word "gospel" by extending it backwards from Jesus' death and resurrection to include the whole public ministry of Jesus from its beginning. The Gospel begins with John the Baptist and the baptism of Jesus by him (1:1–13). The story thus spans Jesus' life from baptism to Good Friday and Easter. This understanding made it possible for the evangelist to include under the heading of "gospel" the material reporting the words and deeds of Jesus which had previously circulated orally. Everything reported—the various deeds and miracles of Jesus' ministry—was thereby understood in terms of the one gospel. By doing this the evangelist did not want merely to retell incidents from the past; it was rather a matter of portraying to the churches who the Lord was whom they confessed in the present. His hidden glory shines forth from his words (4:10–12). And the miracle stories reveal that sickness and evil spirits must retreat now that the savior has entered the scene (3:10–12). The whole portrayal of the ministry of Jesus stands under the sign of the cross (3:6). And Jesus' preaching can only be understood by those to whom the mystery of the kingdom of God has been given (4:11), those who recognize that Jesus of Nazareth, the one who proclaims the dawn of the kingdom of God (1:14–15), is himself the content of the good news (1:1). This is the message that the evangelist wants to pass on, not only among Jews, but to all nations (13:10).

Both Matthew and Luke used the Gospel of Mark as a major source. It is obvious, however, that they composed their writings independently of each other. Both Gospels begin with stories of the birth and childhood of Jesus, but these stories do not agree, since they are based on different traditions (Matthew 1—2//Luke 1—2). While the two gospels differ considerably from each other in these introductory chapters, their description of the public ministry of Jesus begins to agree at the point where they are both dependent on the Marcan account (Mark 1:1//Matt. 3:1//Luke 3:1). The same relationship is observable at the end of the Gospels. The evangelists Matthew and Luke follow the common thread of the Easter story up through the last verse of the Marcan narrative (Mark 16:8//

Matt. 28:8//Luke 24:9), but then go their separate ways, relating different stories of the appearances of the risen one to his disciples (Matt. 28:9–20//Luke 24:13–53). The Gospel of Mark breaks off with the sentence that the women to whom the risen Christ had appeared said nothing to anyone, for they were afraid (16:8). Because this conclusion was considered to be unsatisfactory, as early as the second century a longer ending was appended in which a summary of the different Easter stories is given (16:9–20). This section does not belong to the original text of Mark.

Not only from the outline of the Gospels, but also by a detailed comparison of their contents, one can see that the Gospel of Mark is the oldest of the three. Thus according to Mark 8:29, Peter, the spokesman for the disciples, responds to Jesus' question, "But who do you say that I am?" by saying: "You are the Christ." Both Matthew and Luke take this statement from Mark, but each adds a supplementary explanation. Matt. 16:16 says: "You are the Christ, the Son of the living God," in order to make it absolutely clear that the Messiah is the Son of God. And in Luke 9:20 Peter's answer is, "The Christ of God," in order to leave no doubt that Jesus is God's agent. Both evangelists, therefore, want to explain the text that comes to them in the Gospel of Mark so that it is clearer to their respective readers.

In addition to the Gospel of Mark, both Matthew and Luke were able to use a second source which consisted principally of sayings and parables of Jesus. This is clear from the fact that in many sections of their gospels they agree so closely that they must be dependent on a written collection of the words of Jesus, for example, in the parable of the leaven (Matt. 13:33//Luke 13:20–21), or of the great supper (Matt. 22:1–14//Luke 14:16–24), or the story of the nobleman of Capernaum (Matt. 8:5–13//Luke 7:1–10). This source has not been preserved, but its outline and contents can be reconstructed with some precision by comparing the texts of the Gospels of Matthew and Luke.

The evangelists Matthew and Luke wrote their Gospels around A.D. 90. Both were looking back on the destruction of Jerusalem (Matt. 22:7//Luke 19:43–44; 21:20). The Gospel of John was the last of the four to be written. It presupposes the final separation between Judaism and Christianity, as had happened by the end of the century (John 9:22; 12:42; 16:2). All the same, the Fourth Gospel would like to emphasize that Jesus is the King of Israel (1:49), the Savior of the world (4:42). In this respect the fourth evangelist is not dependent on any of the other Gospels as a source, though he does use traditions which are also incorporated in the other books—for example, the narrative developments in chapter 6: the miraculous feeding of a great crowd, the disciples' trip across the lake, and a speech of Jesus. The evangelist, however, arranges and reformulates these traditions with great freedom, in order to develop his distinctive testimony to Christ for the churches. But when he declares the purpose for which he has written his book, he is in agreement with the other evangelists: "That you may believe that Jesus is the Christ, the Son of God, and that believing you may have life in his name" (20:31).

All the Gospels report Jesus' ministry, suffering, death, and resurrection as the means of calling people to faith. While early Christian letters could adopt a form that was already present and generally known in the ancient world, there was no literary model already available for the Gospels. They are not an example of a later genre of literature, the memoirs or records of the activities of significant personalities. As literary works, the Gospels are a new creation of the Christian church; they utilized the story of Jesus' deeds and ministry, as well as his passion and resurrection, to bear witness to the gospel.

In the second century, these four books—Matthew, Mark, Luke, and John—were brought together into one collection to facilitate their being read aloud in the worship service. Because the one gospel message formed the content of all four Gospel books, they were given titles intended to express their unique character: "The Gospel—according to Matthew, according to Mark, according to Luke, according to John." The good news is one message, but it is expressed in the fourfold witness of the evangelists, each in his own way.

BIBLE

The Bible for Jesus and the first Christian congregations was the Old Testament, which, together with the Jews, they read as Holy Scripture: it declared God's promises and set forth his will and commandments. Then, when early Christian writings appeared in the second half of the first century and the beginning of the second century, a collection of Christian books gradually took their place alongside the writings of the Old Testament and were combined to form the New Testament. Both parts together form the Bible, which is read to this day in all Christian churches.

The writings of the Old Testament are composed in the Hebrew language, except for a few sections of the books of Ezra and Daniel which are written in Aramaic. The Old Testament had already been translated into Greek in pre-Christian times, for there were Greek-speaking people throughout the Mediterranean world. Jesus and his disciples spoke Aramaic. All the New Testament writings, however, are written in Greek. So it is that the sayings and parables of Jesus are available to us only in Greek; they bear the clear marks, however, of having originally been spoken in Aramaic. Since Christian missionaries preached in Greek, when the Old Testament writings were referred to it was always in their Greek translation, as had long been the custom in Judaism also.

No original manuscript of any biblical writing has been preserved; the texts available to us are only copies of copies. The same is true of almost every literary document of antiquity. For no other literary work of the ancient world, however, does there exist so many manuscripts—of such good quality—as resources for the original text as we have for the New Testament. Many ancient writings are known only through copies made in the Middle Ages, so that more than a thousand years exist between the time of their original composition and the oldest preserved manuscript. In contrast, manuscripts of the New Testament are preserved from as early as the second century after Christ, so that only about a hundred years exist between the writing of the New Testament documents and the earliest extant written evidence. The oldest fragment is a single page which contains a few verses from the passion story of the Fourth Gospel. It comes from the early second century and was found in the desert sands of Egypt. This page is separated by only a few decades from the composition of the Fourth Gospel.

People in antiquity wrote mostly on papyrus, an easily perishable writing material. It was made from the pulp of the papyrus plant, by cutting small strips, drying them, and gluing them together. There was no spacing between individual words and sentences. From the time of the emperor Constantine on, Christians were also able to use the more expensive parchment, since they enjoyed the recognition and support of the state. Parchment was made from animal skins worked into a durable writing material. This is why a larger number of biblical manuscripts have been preserved from the fourth century on. Prior to the invention of the printing press, the Bible was repeatedly copied by hand and circulated in manuscripts numbered in the thousands.

The word "Bible" is a Greek word, and means "the Book." As the book of books, the Bible is actually something like a library, for it contains a large number of writings which originated over the span of a millennium. The oldest voices come from the time when Israel moved from the wilderness into Palestine and took possession of the land. They tell how the people, after a long march and many struggles, first gained a foothold in the land. From the time of the beginning of the kingdom in Israel, some very exact reports are preserved: they tell how Israel chose a king, how the kingship then passed from Saul to David, and finally how it came to David's son Solomon (about 1000 B.C.). These stories are told by the very people who, for the most part, experienced the events related in the narratives handed down in the books of Samuel and Kings. From the following centuries we hear the voices of the prophets, beginning with Elijah and Elisha, continuing through the major prophets. We also hear those prophets who announced God's judgment on Israel, which happened with the conquest and destruction of Jerusalem by the Babylonians (586 B.C.). The painful experiences of Israel during the later period of reconstruction in Palestine are dealt with in individual books of the minor prophets. Songs and sayings, rules for living, and gems of wisdom are collected in the books of Psalms and Proverbs, as well as in the other poetic books of the Old Testament.

This comprehensive collection of writings lets us perceive how the people of Israel lived in the presence of their God through the long course of centuries—both in obedience and disobedience.

Even so, God's promise is not nullified by human unfaithfulness.

The final determination of the limits of the collection of Old Testament writings was first made by Jewish scribes at the end of the first century A.D. This collection was identified by the Greek word "canon," which originally meant "measuring stick," "rule," "norm." Those books were acknowledged as Holy Scripture: it contained God's word and command in Law, prophetic preaching, and songs of praise. The Five Books of Moses, containing God's Law, were considered to be separate, forming Israel's first Bible (Torah), soon after the return of the Jews from the Babylonian exile. The collection and canonization of the prophetic books was completed around 200 B.C. The final part of the Old Testament was formed by the poetic books, the largest of which is the Book of Psalms. Thus, by the time of Jesus and the early Christians, the question of which books belong in the Bible was practically settled.

The New Testament documents frequently refer to "the Scriptures," and presuppose that they consist of "the law of Moses and the prophets and the psalms" (Luke 24:44). A few questions were, of course, still being debated among the Jewish scribes. Only after the Song of Solomon was understood to be concerned with the relation of God to Israel, and this interpretation became generally accepted, was it possible to make a positive judgment about the canonical status of this book. And when the observed contradictions between the legal instructions in the book of Ezekiel and the regulations of the Five Books of Moses had been resolved, the canonical authority of this prophet was no longer doubted. In order to make such decisions, the Jewish scribes turned to the Law and its exposition. With the help of this criterion, the distinction was made between the books of Holy Scripture and other books. The Law (Torah) was seen as the center of Scripture: against it all individual statements were to be measured, and they were all to be understood in light of it.

The interpretation of Scripture practiced by the first Christians is clearly distinguished from the understanding of the Old Testament prevalent in Judaism. The early Christians read the biblical books as testimony from and about the Christ who is proclaimed in the gospel. The message of good news which testified to him as Son of God and Lord thus served the Christian community as the key to the understanding of Scripture as a whole. In contrast to that kind of interpretation which used the Law as a guide, having been developed and made binding in the synagogue, early Christians emphasized that the gospel alone could teach us to perceive what God wanted to say to his church through the diverse writings in the Scripture.

In the course of the second century A.D. the Christian community developed the basic components of a canon of New Testament writings. About the middle of the century, an unknown author, of a writing published under the name of the apostle Peter, spoke of "all the letters of our beloved brother Paul" (2 Pet. 3:15–16*). This indicates that he could assume his readers were acquainted with a collection of Paul's letters. As apostolic preaching, they were esteemed among the churches, although already at that time it was perceived that "there are some things in them hard to understand" (3:16). By this time, all four Gospels were also already read throughout Christian communities. In Mark 16:9–20, a later appendage to this Gospel, a summary of the Easter stories of all four Gospels has been collated, in order to bring together their separate messages into one unified story.

The question, however, of which books—in addition to the four Gospels and the letters of Paul—were to be counted as Holy Scripture was not resolved until near the end of the fourth century. In A.D. 367 Bishop Athanasius of Alexandria wrote an Easter letter to his churches. In it he included a list of the twenty-seven books which were to be considered as parts of the New Testament. The size and content of the New Testament has remained firmly fixed since that date. The Latin church adopted the fixation of the canonical books which had been made by the Greek church. "These," wrote Athanasius, "are the springs of salvation, by which the thirsty can be abundantly refreshed. In them alone is the true religious teaching proclaimed. Let no one either add anything or take away anything."

The New Testament, then, is a collection of writings that shows what the first Christians believed and preached—a faith and message by which the church was established and sustained. These writings unanimously testify to the gospel of God's grace, which in Christ is extended to all people of the world. In Christ the Word of God was revealed, a Word that is always conveyed through words spoken by human beings. That Word, preached in a variety of ways, is to be heard wherever the good news of God's grace is proclaimed. It is this news, this gospel, that is the heart and center of Scripture, giving unity to all its parts. The critical norm for this judgment is explained by Martin Luther in his Preface to the letter of James in his translation of the New Testament. "That is the true test by which to judge all books, when we see whether or not they inculcate Christ . . . whatever does not teach Christ is not yet apostolic, even though St. Peter or St. Paul does the teaching. Again, whatever preaches Christ would be apostolic, even if Judas, Annas, Pilate, and Herod were doing it."

With the help of this criterion Luther assigned differing weight to particular biblical writings. The letter of James teaches that one becomes righteous before God by a combination of faith and works (James 2:14–26). These statements stand in contradiction to the Pauline preaching of the justification of the sinner who receives the promise of divine grace by faith alone. This is why Luther designated James as an "epistle of straw." He made similar judgments about the letter to the Hebrews and the Revelation of John. Since the letter to the Hebrews denies the possibility that a sinner who has once received grace and then fallen back into sin can repent a second time and be accepted back into the church (6:4–6; 10:29–30; 12:17), Luther measured this teaching critically by the standard of the apostle's teaching. And because the Revelation of John speaks in visions and symbols instead of preaching the gospel in clear words and plain speech, he attributed no genuine apostolic authority to it. That is why these writings were placed at the end of Luther's translation of the Bible, to indicate that they stood on a lower plane in comparison with the other books.

No other book in world literature has been so widely distributed as the Bible. But it does not begin to speak until it finds willing hearers who will accept its word. As Martin Luther once said, the gospel "is nothing else than a proclaiming, a crying forth of the grace and compassion of God, bought and paid for by the Lord Christ with his own death. And it is really not that which is contained in books and written in letters on paper, but more of an oral proclamation, a living word and voice, which echoes throughout the whole world and is called out in public, so that it can be heard by everyone." This is why the Bible wants to be preached and heard, read and lived.

FOR FURTHER READING

Anderson, Bernhard. *The Living Word of the Bible.* Philadelphia: Westminster Press, 1979.

Beck, Brian E. *Reading the New Testament for Today.* Atlanta: John Knox Press, 1978

The Bible Speaks Again. Minneapolis: Augsburg Publishing House, 1969.

Brueggemann, Walter. *The Bible Makes Sense.* Atlanta: John Knox Press, 1977.

Craddock, Fred B. *The Gospels.* Nashville: Abingdon Press, 1981.

Goodspeed, Edgar J. "The Canon of the New Testament." In *The Interpreter's Bible,* 1:63–71. Edited by George A. Buttrick. 12 vols. Nashville: Abingdon Press, 1954.

Interpreter's Dictionary of the Bible, Supplementary volume. Entry of "Canon of the NT," by A. C. Sundberg, Jr.

——, Supplementary volume. Entry of "Canon of the OT," by D. N. Freedman.

Jeffery, Arthur. "The Canon of the Old Testament." In *The Interpreter's Bible,* 1:32–45. Edited by George A. Buttrick. 12 vols. Nashville: Abingdon Press, 1954.

Keck, Leander. *Taking the Bible Seriously.* Nashville: Abingdon Press, 1979.

Lohse, Eduard. *The Formation of the New Testament.* Nashville: Abingdon Press, 1981.

March, W. Eugene. *Basic Bible Story.* Philadelphia: Geneva Press, 1978.

SCRIPTURE INDEX

OLD TESTAMENT

Genesis
1:27—89
2—90
2:24—90
15:6—83, 86
18—25

Exodus
19:5-6—64
20:4—95
24:3-8—74

Leviticus
16:29-34—44
18:16—12
19:18—40
20:10—92
20:21—12
23:10—103

Deuteronomy
6:5—40
14:22-29—44
23:2-4—64
24:1—93

1 Samuel
10:1—14

2 Samuel
7:11-16—14

1 Kings
2:35—59
17:21—51

2 Kings
4:34—51

Psalms
4:4—63
22—21
22:1—16
22:7-8—16
22:18—16
22:19—16
31:5—16
69:21—16
105:43—63
143—83

Isaiah
7:9—81
28:16—81
29:18-19—52
35:5-6—52
53:4—16

53:5—16
53:6—16
53:7-8—79
53:9—16, 21
53:11—16
53:12—16
62:12—63

Jeremiah
7:11—19
31:31-34—74

Daniel
7:13—15

Hosea
11:1—63

Joel
3:13—32

Micah
5:2-6—11

NEW TESTAMENT